THE

JOY

OF THE

LORD

THE
JOY
OF THE
LORD

CHARLES
SPURGEON

Whitaker House

Unless otherwise indicated, all Scripture quotations are taken from the *King James Version* (KJV) of the Bible.

Scripture quotations marked (RV) are taken from the *Revised Version* of the Holy Bible.

THE JOY OF THE LORD

ISBN: 0-88368-447-0
Printed in the United States of America
Copyright © 1998 by Whitaker House

Whitaker House
30 Hunt Valley Circle
New Kensington, PA 15068

Library of Congress Cataloging-in-Publication Data

Spurgeon, C. H. (Charles Haddon), 1834-1892.
    The joy of the Lord / by Charles Spurgeon.
        p.   cm.
    ISBN 0-88368-447-0 (trade paper)
    1. Jesus Christ—Person and offices. I. Title.
  BT201.S78 1998
  232—dc21   98-10841

1 2 3 4 5 6 7 8 9 10 11 12 13 / 10 09 08 07 06 05 04 03 02 01 00 99 98

Contents

Chapter 1

All Things New

And he that sat upon the throne said,
Behold, I make all things new.
—Revelation 21:5

How pleased we are with things that are new!
Our children's eyes sparkle when we talk
about giving them a new toy or a new book.
Our human nature loves things that are recent because they are like our fleeting lives—suddenly here
for a brief time and then gone. In our love of novelty,
we are all children, for we eagerly demand the news
of the day and are all too ready to rush after new in-
ventions. The Athenians, who spent their time in
nothing else but telling and hearing something new
(Acts 17:21), were by no means unusual; novelty still
fascinates the crowd.

Therefore, I would not be surprised if the words
of our text sound like a pleasant song in your ears,
but I am thankful that their deeper meaning is even
more joyous. The newness that Jesus brings is
bright, clear, heavenly, and enduring.

As Christians, we should not be carried away by a childish love of novelty, for we worship a God who is always the same, and whose years will have no end (Ps. 102:27). In some matters, *"the old is better"* (Luke 5:39). There are certain old things that are so truly new that to exchange them for anything else would be like exchanging old gold for new dross. The old, old Gospel is the newest thing in the world. In its very essence, it is forever the Good News. In the things of God, the old is always new. If anyone presents what seems to be new doctrine and new truth, it is soon perceived that the new dogma is only worn-out heresy cleverly repaired. The so-called discovery in theology is the digging up of a carcass of error that should have been left to rot in oblivion. In the great matter of truth and godliness, we may safely say, *"There is no new thing under the sun"* (Eccl. 1:9).

Yet, there has been so much evil in ourselves and our old natures, so much sin in our lives and our pasts, so much wickedness in our surroundings and old temptations, that we are not distressed by the belief that old things are passing away. Hope springs up at the first sound of such words as these from the lips of our risen and reigning Lord: *"Behold, I make all things new."* It is fitting that things so worn-out and defiled be laid aside and that better things take their places.

The words that Christ speaks to us are truly divine. Listen to them: *"Behold, I."* Who is the great *"I"*? Who else but the eternal Son of God? *"Behold, I make."* Who can create but God, the Maker of heaven and earth? It is His prerogative to make and

8

to destroy. *"Behold, I make all things."* What a range of creating power! Nothing stands outside of that all-encompassing power. *"Behold, I make all things new."* What a splendor of almighty goodness shines out upon our souls! Lord, let us enter into this new universe of Yours. Let us be a part of the *"all things"* that are newly created. May others see the marvels of Your renewing love in us!

Let us thank Jesus as we hear these encouraging words that He speaks from His throne. O Lord, we want to rejoice and be glad forever in what You create. The former troubles are forgotten and are hidden from our eyes because of Your ancient promise, *"Behold, I create new heavens and a new earth: and the former shall not be remembered, nor come into mind"* (Isa. 65:17).

I am going to write a little about the great transformation spoken of in the text: *"I make all things new."* Then I will go on to describe the earnest call in the text to consider that transformation: *"He that sat upon the throne said, Behold."* In other words, He said, "Pay attention to it, consider it, look at it!" *"Behold, I make all things new."* Oh, for an outpouring of the Holy Spirit while I discuss this theme and while you read about it!

THE GREAT TRANSFORMATION

Here is one of the greatest truths that ever came from the lips of Jesus: *"Behold, I make all things new."* Let us gaze upon the great transformation.

This renewing work has been in our Lord's hands since long ago. Originally, we were under the

9

old covenant, and when our first father and covenantal head, Adam, broke that covenant, we were ruined by his fatal violation. The substance of the old covenant that God made with Adam was this: "If you keep my command, you will live, and your posterity will live. But if you eat from the tree that I have forbidden you to eat from, you will die, and all your posterity in you will die."

As we know, Adam ate the forbidden fruit, and the tremendous Fall destroyed both our Paradise and ourselves. We were broken in pieces, seriously wounded, and even killed. We died in Adam, as far as spiritual life is concerned, and our state of death revealed itself in an inward tendency to evil that reigned in our members. We were like Ezekiel's deserted infant, unclothed and unwashed, left in our uncleanness to die, but the Son of God passed by and saw us in the greatness of our ruin (Ezek. 16:1–14). In His wondrous love, our Lord Jesus put us under a new covenant, a covenant in which He became the Second Adam, a covenant in which God said to His Son, "If You will live in perfect obedience and vindicate My justice, then those who are in You will not perish, but they will live because You live."

Now, our Lord Jesus, our Surety and covenantal Head, has fulfilled His portion of the covenant, and the compact stands as a bond of pure promise without condition or risk. Those who are participants in that covenant cannot invalidate it, for it never did depend on them, but only on Him who was and is their covenantal Head and Representative before God. Of Jesus the demand was made, and He met it. By Him, man's side of the covenant was undertaken and fulfilled, and now no condition remains; the covenant is made up solely of promises that are unconditional and sure to all who are in Christ. Today, believers are not under the covenant "If you do this, you will live," but under the new covenant that says, *"Their sins and their iniquities will I remember no more"* (Heb. 8:12). The new covenant is not "Do and live," but "Live and do." The new covenant is not of merit and reward, but of free grace producing a holy lifestyle as the result of gratitude. What law could not do, grace has accomplished.

We must never forget this basis of everything, this making all things new by the fashioning of a new covenant. By it, we have been released from the bondage of the law and the ruin of the Fall, and we have entered into the liberty of Christ, into acceptance with God, and into the boundless joy of being saved in the Lord with an everlasting salvation. We *"shall not be ashamed nor confounded world without end"* (Isa. 45:17).

If you know the Lord, I exhort you to thoroughly study that word *covenant.* If you do not yet know the Lord, I encourage you to study that word as soon as you come to know Him. It is a key word that opens the treasures of revelation. He who properly understands the difference between the two covenants has the foundation of sound theology laid in his mind. This understanding is the clue to many perplexities, the "open sesame" of many mysteries. Jesus makes *"all things new,"* beginning with the bringing in of a better hope through a better covenant.

The foundation having been made new, the Lord Jesus Christ has set before us a new way of life, which grows out of that covenant. The old way of life was "If you want to enter into life, keep the commandments." The commandments are perfect, holy, just, and good (Rom. 7:12). But, alas, dear friend, you and I have broken the commandments. We dare not say that we have kept the Ten Commandments our whole lives; on the contrary, our consciences compel us to confess that in spirit and in heart, if not in act, we have continually broken the law of God. Therefore, we are under sin and condemnation, and there is no hope for us to be saved by the works of the law.

For this reason, the Gospel sets before us another way, and says, *"It is of faith, that it might be by grace"* (Rom. 4:16), and *"Believe on the Lord Jesus Christ, and thou shalt be saved"* (Acts 16:31). Therefore, we read of being *"justified by faith"* (Rom. 3:28), and being made acceptable to God by faith. To be *"justified"* means to be made truly righteous. Though we were guilty in ourselves, we are regarded as just because of what the Lord Jesus Christ has done for us. Thus, we fell into condemnation through another, and we rise into justification through Another. It is written, *"By his knowledge shall my righteous servant justify many; for he shall bear their iniquities"* (Isa. 53:11), and this verse is fulfilled in all those who believe in the Lord Jesus and receive eternal life.

Our path to eternal glory is the road of faith: *"The just shall live by faith"* (Rom. 1:17). We are *"accepted in the beloved"* (Eph. 1:6) when we believe in the One whom God has set forth to be our righteousness. *"By the deeds of the law there shall no flesh be justified in his sight"* (Rom. 3:20), but we are *"justified freely by his grace through the redemption that is in Christ Jesus"* (v. 24).

What a blessing it is for you and for me that Jesus has made all things new in this respect! I am glad that I do not have to say, "My dear reader, do this and do that, and you will be saved." You would not do as you were commanded, for your fallen nature is weak and wicked. But I can say to you,

Lay your deadly doing down, down at Jesus' feet;
Stand in Him, in Him alone, gloriously complete.

I trust that you will accept this most gracious way of salvation. It is most glorious to God and safe for you. Do not neglect so great a salvation (Heb. 2:3). After you have believed and have received life, you will do all kinds of holy deeds as the result of your new life, but do not attempt them with a view to earning life. Prompted no longer by the servile and selfish motive of saving yourself, but by gratitude for the fact that you are saved, you will rise to virtue and true holiness. Faith has given us an irreversible salvation, and now, because of the love that we have for our Savior, we must obey Him and become *"zealous of good works"* (Titus 2:14).

By grace, every believer is brought into a new relationship with God. Let us rejoice in this: *"Thou art no more a servant, but a son; and if a son, then an heir of God through Christ"* (Gal. 4:7). Oh, you who are now a believing child, you were an unbelieving servant a little while ago! Or, perhaps you are still an unbelieving servant; if you are, I tell you to expect your wages. Alas, your service has not been true

13

service, but rebellion; and if you get no more wages than you deserve, you will be cast away forever. You ought to be thankful to God that He has not paid you yet, that *"he hath not dealt with* [you] *after* [y]*our sins; nor rewarded* [you] *according to* [y]*our iniquities"* (Ps. 103:10).

Don't you know, you unbelieving servant, what is likely to happen to you as a servant? What would you yourself do with a bad servant? You would say to him, "There are your wages. Go." *"The servant abideth not in the house for ever"* (John 8:35). You, too, will be driven from your hypocritical profession of faith. Your period of probation will end, and where will you go? The wilderness of destruction lies before you!

"Behold, I make all things new," says Jesus. Indeed, He makes His people into sons. When we are made sons, do we work for wages? We have no desire for any present payment, for our Father says to us, *"Son, thou art ever with me, and all that I have is thine"* (Luke 15:31). Moreover, we have the inheritance given to us by the covenant. We cannot demand a servant's wages, because we already have all that our Father possesses. He has given us Himself and His all-sufficiency for our everlasting portion; what more can we desire? He will never drive us from His house. Never has our great Father disowned one of His sons. It cannot be. His loving heart is too closely involved with His own adopted ones. That near and dear relationship that is manifested in adoption and regeneration binds the child of God to the great Father's heart in such a way that He will never cast him away or allow him to perish. I

rejoice in the fact that we are no longer servants, but sons. *"Behold,"* says Christ, *"I make all things new."*

The Holy Spirit has put within us a new life, with all the new feelings, the new desires, and the new works that go with it. The tree has been made new, and the fruits are new as a result. The same Spirit of God who taught us that we were ruined in our old state of sin led us gently by the hand until we came to the new covenantal promise, looked to Jesus, and saw in Him the full atonement for sin. Happy discovery for us! It was the kindling of new life in us. The moment that we trusted in Jesus, a new life darted into our spirits. I am not going to say which comes first: the new birth, faith, or repentance. When a wheel moves, no one can say which spoke moves first; it moves as a whole. The moment the divine life comes into the heart, we believe; the moment we believe, the eternal life is there. Then we no longer live according to the lusts of the world, but we live by faith in the Son of God, who loved us and gave Himself for us (Gal. 2:20).

Our spiritual life is a newborn thing, the creation of the Spirit of life. We have, of course, the natural life that is sustained by food and that is evidenced by the fact that we are breathing, but there is another life within us that is not seen by others and is not fed by earthly provisions. We are conscious of having been spiritually awakened. We were dead once, and we know it; but now we have passed from death into life (John 5:24), and we know this just as certainly. A new and higher motive sways us now, for we do not seek self, but God. A new hand steers our ship in a new course. We feel new desires,

15

to which we were strangers in our former state. New fears are mighty within us—holy fears that once we would have ridiculed. New hopes are in us, bright and sure, such as we did not even desire to have when we lived a mere carnal life. We are not what we were; we are new, and we have begun a new life. I admit that we are not what we will be, but assuredly, we are not what we used to be.

As for myself, my consciousness of being a new man in Christ Jesus is often as sharp and crisp as my consciousness of being in existence. I know that I am not solely what I was by my first birth. I feel within myself another life—a second and a higher vitality—that often has to contend with my lower self, and by that very contention makes me conscious of its existence. This new life is, from day to day, gathering strength and winning the victory. It has its hand on the throat of the old sinful nature, and it will eventually trample it like dust beneath its feet. I feel this new life within me; do you? If you feel it, I know that you can say that Jesus Christ, who sits on the throne, makes all things new. Blessed be His name. We needed the Lord Himself to make people such as we are new. No one but a Savior on the throne could accomplish it; therefore, let Him have the glory for it.

Perhaps Jesus Christ has not only made you new, but has made everything new to you. "Oh," one woman said when she was converted, "either the world is greatly changed, or else I am." Why, either you and I are turned upside down, or the world is. We used to think that the world is wise, but we think that it is very foolish now! We used to think of it as a brave, glad world that showed us real happiness, but we are no longer deceived. *"The world is crucified unto me,"* Paul said in Galatians 6:14, and perhaps you can say the same. To believers, the world is like a vile criminal who is taken out and hanged. Meanwhile, there is no love lost, for the world thinks much the same of us, and we can agree with Paul when he said, *"I* [am crucified] *unto the world"* (v. 14).

Grace greatly transforms everything in our little world! In our hearts, there is a new heaven and a new earth. What a change in our joys! We blush to think about what we used to enjoy, but we enjoy heavenly things now. We are equally ashamed of our former hates and prejudices, but these have vanished once and for all. Why, now we love the very things we once despised, and our hearts run after the things that they once detested. How different the Bible seems now! Blessed book, it is exactly the same, but, oh, how differently we read it. The mercy seat of God, what a different place it is now! Our wretched, formal prayers—if we bothered to pray at all—what a mockery they were! But now we draw near to God and speak to Him with delight. We have access to Him by the *"new and living way"* (Heb. 10:20). The house of God, how different it is from what it used to be! We love to be found within its walls, and we feel delighted to join in the praises of the Lord.

After a recent church service, I shook the hand of a man who does not often hear me preach. He expressed to me his boundless delight in listening to the doctrine of the grace of God, and he added,

"Surely your congregation must be made of stone." "Why?" I asked. He replied, "If they were not, they would all get up and shout 'hallelujah' when you are preaching such a glorious Gospel. I wanted very much to shout, but since everybody else was quiet, I held my tongue." I thought he was a wise man for remaining silent, yet I am not surprised if men who have tasted God's grace do feel like crying out for joy.

Why shouldn't we lift up our voices in His praise? We will. He has put a new song into our mouths (Ps. 40:3), and we must sing it. *"The mountains and the hills...break forth before* [us] *into singing"* (Isa. 55:12), and we cannot be silent. Praise is our ever new delight. In praise, we will compete with angels and archangels, for they are not so indebted to grace as we are.

> Never did angels taste above
> Redeeming grace and dying love.

But we have tasted these precious things, and unto God we will lift up our loudest song forever and forever.

The process that I have roughly described as taking place in believers is going on in the physical world in other forms. All time is groaning, providence is working, grace is striving, the whole creation is giving birth, and all for one end—the bringing forth of the new and better age. It is coming. It is coming. John did not write the following in vain:

> *And I saw a new heaven and a new earth: for*
> *the first heaven and the first earth were passed*

*away; and there was no more sea. And I John
saw the holy city, new Jerusalem, coming
down from God out of heaven, prepared as a
bride adorned for her husband. And I heard a
great voice out of heaven saying, Behold, the
tabernacle of God is with men, and he will
dwell with them, and they shall be his people,
and God himself shall be with them, and be
their God. And God shall wipe away all tears
from their eyes; and there shall be no more
death, neither sorrow, nor crying, neither shall
there be any more pain: for the former things
are passed away. And he that sat upon the
throne said, Behold, I make all things new.
And he said unto me, Write: for these words
are true and faithful.* (Rev. 21:1–5)

What a prospect all this opens up to the believer!
Our future is glorious; we must not let our present
be gloomy.

AN EARNEST CALL

Next, in the text, there is an earnest call for us
to consider this work of our Lord. He who sits on the
throne says, *"Behold, I make all things new."* Why
should He call on us to behold this? All His works
deserve study. *"The works of the LORD are great,
sought out of all them that have pleasure therein"*
(Ps. 111:2). Whatever the Lord does is full of wisdom, and the wise will look into His works. But
when the Lord Himself sets up a light and calls us to
pause and look, we cannot help but respond.

I think that the Lord Jesus Christ specifically calls us to consider the fact that He makes all things new, so that we may be comforted, regardless of our condition.

To the Unsaved

First, this verse is a comfort to the unsaved. If the Lord Jesus makes all things new, then a new birth is possible for you, dear friend, even though you have a wrong state of heart and your sins are upon you, clutching you tightly. There is enough light in your soul for you to know that you are in darkness, and you are saying to yourself, "Oh, if only I could attain better things! I hear people praise God for what Christ has done for them. Can He do the same for me?" Listen! He who sits on the throne says in infinite graciousness to you on the trash heap, *"Behold, I make all things new."* There is nothing so old that He cannot make it new— nothing so ingrained and habitual that He cannot change it.

Don't you know, dear heart, that the Spirit of God has regenerated men and women just as far gone as you are? They were as deep in sin and as hardened by habit as you could ever be. They thought that they were hopeless, just as you think that you are. Yet the Spirit of God carried out the will of the Lord Christ and made them new. Why shouldn't He make you new? May every thief know that the dying thief entered heaven by faith in Jesus. May everyone who has been a great sinner remember how Manasseh received a new heart and repented of his evil deeds. (See 2 Chronicles 33:1–13.) Let everyone who has left the paths of purity remember how the woman who was a sinner loved much because she had been forgiven much. (See Luke 7:37–48.)

I cannot doubt the possibility of your salvation, my dear friend, whenever I think of my own. A more determined, obstinate rebel could scarcely have existed. Because I was a child and was kept from gross outward sin by holy restraints, I had a powerful inner nature that would not tolerate control. I rebelliously strove hard. I labored to win heaven by self-righteousness, and this is as real a rebellion as open sin. But, oh, the grace of God, how it can tame us! How it can turn us! With no bit or bridle, but with a blessed tenderness, it turns us according to its pleasure. Oh, anxious one, it can turn you! Therefore, I want to drop this truth into your mind (and may the Spirit of God drop it into your heart): you can be born again. The Lord can work a radical change in you. He who sits on the throne can do for you what you cannot do for yourself. He made you once, and even though you became marred by sin, He can make you new again. He says, *"Behold, I make all things new."*

To Those Who Want a New Life

This verse is also a comfort to those who desire to lead a new life. To have a new life, you must be new yourself; for as the man is, so his life will be. If the fountain is contaminated, the streams cannot be pure. Renewal must begin with the heart. Dear friend, the Lord Jesus Christ is able to make your life entirely new. I have seen many people transformed into new parents and new children. Friends have exclaimed in amazement, "What a change in John! What a difference in Ellen!" I have seen men become new husbands and women become new wives. They are the same people, yet not the same. Grace works a very deep, striking, and lasting change. Ask someone who has seen a member of his household converted whether the transformation has not been marvelous. Christ makes new employees, new supervisors, new friends, new brothers, new sisters. The Lord can so change us that we hardly know ourselves.

He can change you who now despair of yourself. Oh, dear heart, it is not necessary for you to go downward in evil until you descend to hell. There is a hand that can pull you in the opposite direction. It would be an amazing thing if Niagara Falls were to flow backward, ascending instead of descending. It would be an incredible thing if the St. Lawrence River were to run backward to Lake Ontario. Yet, God could do even these things. Likewise, He can reverse the course of your fallen nature and make you act like a new person. He can stop the tide of your raging passion. He can make someone who is like a devil become like an angel of God, for He says this from the throne of His eternal majesty: *"Behold, I make all things new."* Come and lay yourself down at His feet, and ask Him to make you new. I implore you, do this at once!

"Well, I am going to mend myself," some people say. "I have taken a pledge that I will be honest, moral, and religious." This is a commendable decision, but what will come of it? You will break your resolutions; you will not be made any better by your attempts at reform. If you go into the business of mending yourself, you will be like the man who had an old gun. He took it to the gunsmith, and the gunsmith said, "Well, this would make a very good gun if it had a new lock, a new stock, and a new barrel." Likewise, mending would make you a very good person, if you could get a new heart, a new life, and an altogether new self, so that there was not one bit of the old self left.

You can depend on it that it is a great deal easier for God to make you new than to mend you, for the fact is that *"the carnal mind is enmity against God"* (Rom. 8:7). The carnal mind is not reconciled to God; indeed, it cannot be. Therefore, mending will not do; you must be made new. *"Ye must be born again"* (John 3:7). What is needed is for you to be made a new creation in Christ Jesus. You must be dead with Christ, buried with Christ, and risen again in Him (Rom. 6:4). Then all will be well, for He will have made all things new. I ask God to bless these feeble words of mine and use them to help some of His chosen out of the darkness of their fears.

To the Weary Christian

There are children of God who need this text, *"Behold, I make all things new."* They sigh because they often grow dull and weary in the ways of God and therefore need daily renewing. A fellow believer said to me some time ago, "Dear pastor, I frequently

...ry sleepy in my walk with God. I seem to lose ...reshness of it. By about Saturday I feel espe- ...lly dull." Then he added, "But as for you, when- ever I hear you, you seem to be alive and full of fresh energy." "My dear brother," I said, "that is because you do not know much about me." That was all I was able to say just then.

I thank God for keeping me near Himself. But I am as weak, as stale, and as unprofitable as any other believer. I say this with much shame—shame for myself and shame for the brother who led me to make the confession. We are both wrong. Since all our fresh springs are in God (Ps. 87:7), we ought to be full of new life all the time. Every minute, our love for Christ ought to be as if it were newborn. Our zeal for God ought to be as fresh as if we had just begun to delight in Him. "Yes, but it is not," most Christians would say, and I am sorry I cannot contradict them. After a few months, a vigorous young Christian begins to cool down. Likewise, those who have walked in the ways of God for a long time find that final perseverance must be a miracle if it is ever to be accomplished, for they tire and grow faint.

Well now, dear friend, why do you and I ever get stale and flat? Why do we sing,

> Dear Lord, and shall we ever live
> At this poor dying rate?

Why do we have to cry,

> In vain we tune our formal songs,
> In vain we strive to rise;
> Hosannas languish on our tongues,
> And our devotion dies?

Why, it is because we stray away from the One who says, *"Behold, I make all things new."* The way to perpetual newness and freshness is to keep going to Christ, just as we did when we were first saved.

An even better way is never to leave Him, but to stand forever at the foot of the cross, delighting in His all-sufficient sacrifice. Those who are full of the joy of the Lord never grow weary of life. Those who walk in the light of His countenance can say of the Lord Jesus, *"Thou hast the dew of thy youth"* (Ps. 110:3), and that dew falls on those who dwell with Him. Oh, I am sure that if we would maintain perpetual communion with Him, we would enjoy a perpetual stream of delights.

> Immortal joys come streaming down,
> Joys, like His griefs, immense, unknown.

But these joys come only from Him. We will remain young if we stay with the ever young Beloved, whose hair is black as a raven (Song 5:11). He says, and He fulfills the saying, *"Behold, I make all things new."*

He can make that next sermon of yours, my fellow minister, quite new and interesting. He can make that prayer meeting no longer a dreary affair, but quite a new thing to you and all the people. My dear sister, the next time you go to your Sunday school class, the Lord can cause you to feel as if you had just started teaching yesterday. Then you will not be at all tired of your godly work; instead, you will love it better than ever. And you, my dear brother, preaching at the street corner, where you are often interrupted, perhaps with foul language, you will feel pleased with your position of self-denial. Getting near to Christ, you will partake of His joy, and that joy will be your strength, your freshness, the newness of your life. May God grant to us that we may drink of the eternal fountains, so that we may forever overflow.

There may be someone reading this who knows that he is living on a very low plane of spiritual life, but also knows that the Lord can raise him to a new level. Many Christians seem to dwell in the marshes. If you ever travel through the valleys of Switzerland, you will find yourself getting feverish and heavy in spirit, and you will see many who are mentally or physically afflicted. However, if you climb the sides of the hills, ascending into the Alps, you will not see that kind of thing in the pure, fresh air. Unfortunately, many Christians are of the sickly valley breed. Oh, that they could get up to the high mountains and be strong!

If you have been in bondage all your life, I declare that you do not need to stay there any longer. Jesus has the power to make all things new and to lift you into new delights. It might seem like a resurrection from the dead to you, but it is within the power of that pierced hand to lift you right out of doubt, fear, despondency, spiritual lethargy, and weakness, and to make you now, from this day forward, *strong in the Lord, and in the power of his might*" (Eph. 6:10).

Now breathe a prayer, dear brother, dear sister, to the One who makes all things new: "Lord, make Your poor, spiritually sick child strong and spiritually healthy." Oh, what a blessing it would be for some

Christian workers if God would make them strong! The whole church would be better because of the way in which the Lord would help them to do their work. Why should you be living on pennies and starving yourself when your Father would cause you to live like a prince of royal blood if you would only trust Him? I am persuaded that most of us are beggars when we could be millionaires in spiritual things. And here is our strength for rising to a nobler state of mind: *"Behold, I make all things new."*

To the Afflicted Christian

There is another application of this truth. Someone may be saying, "Oh, I do not know what to make of myself. I have had a hard time lately. Everything seems to have gone wrong. My family causes me great anxiety. My business is a thorny maze. My own health is precarious. I dread this year. In fact, I dread everything." We will not go on with that lamentation, but we will hear the encouraging word, *"Behold, I make all things new."* The Lord, in answer to believing prayer, and especially in answer to your full submission to His will, is able to make all your surroundings new. I have known the Lord to turn darkness into light all of a sudden, and to take away the sackcloth and the ashes from His dear children, for *"he doth not afflict willingly nor grieve the children of men"* (Lam. 3:33).

Sometimes all our worry is mere discontentment, and when the child of God gets himself right, these imaginary troubles vanish like the morning mist. But when the troubles are real, God can just as easily change your condition, dear child of God, as He can turn His hand. He can make your harsh and ungodly husband become gentle and gracious. He can bring your children to the place where they will bow at the family altar and rejoice with you in Christ. He can cause your business to prosper. Or, if He does not do that, He can strengthen your back to bear the burden of your daily cross.

Oh, it is wonderful how different a thing becomes when it is taken to God. But you want to make it all new yourself, and you fret and worry; you torture, trouble, and burden yourself. Why not stop that, and in humble prayer, take the matter to the Lord and say, "Lord, come to my aid, for You have said, *'I make all things new.'* Make my circumstances new"? He is certainly able to free you from your captivity.

To Those Anxious about Unsaved Loved Ones

There is one more application, and that is that the Lord can convert those dear unsaved loved ones about whom you have been so anxious. The Lord who makes all things new can hear your prayers. At a prayer meeting that I attended recently, a dear brother prayed that God would save his relatives. Then another prayed with great tenderness for his children. I know that his prayer came from an aching heart. Some of you have heartbreakers at home; may the Lord break their hearts—humbling and softening them so that they will come to Him. You are grieved and troubled because you hear the person you hold the dearest blaspheming the God you love.

You know that your loved ones are Sabbath-breakers, and utterly godless, and you tremble for their eternal fate.

Certain people attend my church who are not saved. I can say of them that I never stand behind the pulpit without looking to their pews to see whether they are there and without praying to God for them. I forget a great many who are saved, but I always pray for these unsaved ones. And they will be brought in, I feel assured, but, oh, that it may be soon!

I liked what one man said at a recent service when his brother was introduced to the church. Wondering about his brother's conversion, I asked, "Were you surprised to see him converted?" He said, "I would have been very much surprised if he had not been." "But why, my dear brother?" I asked. "Because I asked the Lord to convert him, and I kept on praying that he would be converted. I would have been very surprised if he had not been." That is the right sort of faith. I would be very surprised if some of the unsaved who attend my church, time after time, are not converted. They will be, blessed be God. I will give Him no rest until He answers me.

But if you are unsaved, aren't you praying for yourself? Don't you agree with the prayers of your Christian friends and relatives who are praying for you? Oh, I trust that you do. But, even if you do not, they will still pray for you. Even if you are opposed to their intercessions and are even angry with them, they will undoubtedly pray all the more. They intend to have you won for Jesus, by the grace of God, and you may as well come sooner rather than later. They are determined to see you in the church confessing your faith in Jesus. They will never let you go, neither will they cease from their persistent prayers, until they get an answer from the throne, and see you saved. Oh, that you would yield to the One who can make a new creation out of you (2 Cor. 5:17). May God grant that you will!

May the Lord answer my prayers now, for Jesus' sake, for I seek the salvation of every reader of this book.

Chapter 2

This Year Also

He spake also this parable; a certain man
had a fig tree planted in his vineyard; and he came
and sought fruit thereon, and found none. Then said he
unto the dresser of his vineyard, Behold, these three
years I come seeking fruit on this fig tree, and find
none: cut it down; why cumbereth it the ground? And
he answering said unto him, Lord, let it alone this year
also, till I shall dig about it, and dung it: and if it
bear fruit, well: and if not, then after that
thou shalt cut it down.
—Luke 13:6–9

The interceding vinedresser pleaded for the fruitless fig tree, *"Let it alone this year also,"* securing for it another year. During that year, it would have to bear fruit, or else it would be cut down. Unlike people, trees and fruit-bearing plants have a natural way of marking a year. Evidently the tree's year came to its close when it was time to seek fruit on it, and another year commenced when the vinedresser began once again his digging

31

and pruning. But men are such barren things that their fruit-bearing marks no particular periods, and it becomes necessary to make artificial divisions of time for them. There seems to be no set period for man's spiritual harvest or vintage, or if there is, the sheaves and the clusters do not come in their season. Therefore, it is necessary for us to say to one another, "Let us make this the beginning of a new year."

A LOOK AT THE PAST

Look back over the past year of your life and examine it, deliberately and honestly. In the parable of the barren fig tree, there had been former years of grace. It was not the first time that the vinedresser was made aware of the fig tree's failure. It was not the first time that the owner came seeking figs in vain. In the same way, God, who gives us *"this year also,"* has given us others before it. His sparing mercy is no novelty; His patience has already been taxed by our provocations.

First came our youthful years, when even a little fruit for God is especially sweet to Him. How did we spend them? Did we spend all of our strength on sinful pleasures? If so, we should mourn that wasted vigor, that life misspent, that sin exceedingly multiplied. Nevertheless, He who saw us misuse those golden months of youth gives us *"this year also."* We should enter it with a holy jealousy, lest the strength and fervency that are left to us be allowed to flow into the same wasteful avenues as before.

Upon the heels of our youthful years came the years of young adulthood, when we started a family

32

and put out roots. Fruit yielded during that time also would have been precious. Did we bear any? Did we present unto the Lord a basket of summer fruit? Did we offer Him the firstfruits of our strength? If we did so, we should adore the grace that so early saved us; but if not, the past chides us, and, lifting an admonishing finger, it warns us not to let *"this year also"* follow the same path as the rest of our lives. He who has wasted both youth and early adulthood has surely been foolish enough; he has spent enough time following the desires of his flesh. It would be an overflow of wickedness to allow *"this year also"* to be trodden down in the service of sin.

Many of you are now in the prime of life, and many years of your lives are already spent. Do you still need to confess that your years are being eaten up by the grasshopper and the cankerworm (Joel 1:4)? Have you reached midlife and still do not know where you are going? Are you fools at forty? Are you half a century old by the calendar and yet far away from the years of wisdom? How unfortunate that there are men over fifty years old who are still without knowledge! Unsaved at sixty, unregenerate at seventy, unawakened at eighty, unrenewed at ninety—each and every one of these phrases is startling! Perhaps these phrases will startle and awaken someone who is reading this, but, on the other hand, that person might just gloss over them. Continuance in evil breeds hardness of heart, and when the soul has been sleeping in indifference for a long time, it is hard to arouse it from its deadly slumber.

The sound of the words *"this year also"* makes some of us remember years of great mercy, sparkling and flashing with delight. Were those years laid at the Lord's feet? Were they like the horses' silver bells that were engraved with the words, "*HOLINESS UNTO THE LORD*" (Zech. 14:20)? If not, how will we explain our neglect if "*this year also*" is musical with joyful mercy and yet spent in the ways of carelessness?

"*This year also.*" These words cause some of us to recall our years of sharp affliction, when we were indeed dug around and fertilized. What were those years like? God was doing great things for us, cultivating carefully and expensively, caring for us very much and very wisely. Did we give back to God according to the benefits we received from Him? Did we rise from the bed of affliction with more patience and gentleness, weaned from the world and welded to Christ? Did we produce clusters of grapes to reward the Vinedresser? Let us not refuse to answer these questions of self-examination, for this year may be another of those years of trial, another season of the furnace and the crucible. May the Lord grant that the coming tribulation take more chaff out of us than any tribulation before it, leaving the wheat cleaner and better.

A new year reminds us of opportunities for usefulness that have come and gone, and of unfulfilled resolutions that have blossomed, only to fade. Will "*this year also*" be like those that have gone before it? Shouldn't we hope for more grace so that we may build upon grace already gained? And shouldn't we seek power to turn our poor sickly promises into robust action?

Looking back on the past, we lament our foolish actions. We do not want to be held captive by them *"this year also."* At the same time, we adore God's forgiving mercy, His preserving providence, His boundless generosity, and His divine love; and we hope to be partakers of them *"this year also."*

A GIFT OF MERCY

The text also mentions a mercy. Because of the vinedresser's great goodness, the tree that was merely taking up space was allowed to stand for another year. Prolonged life should always be regarded as a gift of mercy. We must view *"this year also"* as a grant from infinite grace. It is wrong to speak as if we cared nothing for life, as if we looked upon our being here on earth as torture or punishment. We are here *"this year also"* as the result of love's pleadings and to pursue love's purposes.

The wicked individual should consider that the Lord's longsuffering points to his salvation, and he should permit the cords of love to draw him to it. Oh, that the Holy Spirit would make the blasphemer, the Sabbath-breaker, and the openly immoral to feel what a wonder it is that their lives are prolonged *"this year also"*! Are they spared to curse and riot and defy their Maker? Should this be the only fruit of patient mercy? Shouldn't the procrastinator who has put off the messenger of heaven with his delays and half promises be amazed that he is allowed to see *"this year also"*? How is it that the Lord has borne with him and has put up with his vacillations and hesitations? Is this year of grace to be spent in the same manner? Short-lived convictions, hasty commitments, and speedy apostasies—are these to be the tiresome story over and over again? The startled conscience, the tyrant passion, the smothered emotion—are these to be the tokens of yet another year?

May God forbid that any one of us should hesitate and delay throughout *"this year also."* Infinite pity holds back the ax of justice. Will His mercy be insulted by the repetition of the sins that caused wrath's instrument to be raised? What can be more tormenting to the heart of goodness than indecision? May the Lord's prophet become impatient and cry, *"How long halt ye between two opinions?"* (1 Kings 18:21). May God Himself push for a decision and demand an immediate reply. Oh, undecided soul, will you swing much longer between heaven and hell, and act as if it were hard to choose between the slavery of Satan and the liberty of the great Father's home of love? *"This year also,"* will you delay in defiance of justice, and pervert the generosity of mercy into a license for still further rebellion? *"This year also,"* must divine love be made an occasion for continued sin? Oh, do not act so wickedly, so contrary to every noble instinct, so injuriously to your own best interests.

The believer, on the other hand, is kept out of heaven *"this year also"* because of God's love, not His anger. There are people who need him to remain on earth. Some need him to help them on their way to heaven, and others need his instruction to lead them to the Redeemer's feet. Many saints do not have their heaven prepared for them yet, because their nearest companions have not yet arrived there, and their spiritual children have not yet gathered there in sufficient numbers to give them a thoroughly heavenly welcome. They must wait *"this year also,"* so that their rest may be even more glorious, and so that the additional souls that they win to Christ may give them greater joy. Surely, for the sake of souls, for the delight of glorifying our Lord, and for the increase of the jewels in our heavenly crowns, we may be glad to wait below *"this year also."*

THE LIMITATIONS OF MERCY

I want to emphasize that the expression *"this year also"* implies a limit. The vinedresser asked for a reprieve of no longer than one year. If his digging and fertilizing should prove unsuccessful, he would plead no more, and the tree would be cut down.

Even when Jesus is the pleader, the request of mercy has its boundaries and limits. We will not be left alone and allowed to needlessly take up space forever. If we will not repent, we must perish. If we will not be benefited by the spade, we must fall by the ax.

There will be a last year for each one of us. Therefore, let each one say to himself, "Is this year my last?" If it were to be the last for me, I would prepare to deliver the Lord's message with all my soul and to tell my fellowmen to be reconciled to God. Dear friend, is this year to be your last? Are you ready to see the curtain rise upon eternity? Are you now prepared to hear the midnight cry and to enter into the marriage supper (Matt. 25:6; Rev. 19:7–9)? The Judgment and all that will follow it are most surely the heritage of every person. Blessed are they who by faith in Jesus are able to face the judgment seat of God without a thought of terror.

Even if we live to be counted among the oldest inhabitants of the earth, we must depart at last. There must come an end, and we will hear the Lord say, *"Thus saith the LORD...this year thou shalt die"* (Jer. 28:16). So many have gone before us, and are going every hour, that no man should need any other reminder that we must die. Yet, man is so eager to forget his own mortality, and thereby to forfeit his hopes of bliss, that we cannot bring it too often before the mind's eye. Oh, mortal man, think! *"Prepare to meet thy God"* (Amos 4:12), for you must meet Him. Seek the Savior; yes, seek Him before another sunset.

"This year also"—and this may be the last year—the Cross is once again uplifted as the lighthouse of the world, the one light to which no eye can look in vain. Oh, that millions would look that way and live. Soon the Lord Jesus will come a second time, and then the blaze of His throne will replace the mild radiance of His cross. The Judge will be seen rather than the Redeemer. Now He saves, but then He will destroy. Let us hear His voice at this moment. Let us be eager to avail ourselves of this gracious season. Let us believe in Jesus this day, since it may be our last. Hear these pleadings for your soul's sake, and live.

Chapter 3

Growing in the Lord

But grow in grace, and in the knowledge of our
Lord and Saviour Jesus Christ. To him be
glory both now and for ever. Amen.
                    —2 Peter 3:18

Beloved, we are perpetually in danger. Where can we go to escape from peril? Where can we go to avoid temptation? If we venture into business, worldliness is there. If we retire to our homes, trials are there. One would imagine that in the green pastures of the Word of God, there would be perfect security for God's sheep. Surely no lion is there; surely no ferocious beast can walk there! Unfortunately, it is not so. Even while we are reading the Bible, we are still exposed to peril. It is not that the truth is dangerous, but that our corrupt hearts can find poison in the very flowers of paradise.

Notice what Peter said about the writings of Paul: *"In which are some things hard to be understood"* (2 Pet. 3:16). And mark the danger to which we are exposed: *"Which they that are unlearned and unstable wrest, as they do also the other scriptures, unto their own destruction"* (v. 16). We can distort even the Word of God to our own destruction. With the Bible before our eyes, we can still commit sin. Pondering over the holy words of inspired Scripture, we can receive a deadly wound from *"the error of the wicked"* (v. 17). Even at the horns of the altar (Exod. 27:1–2; 1 Kings 1:50), we still need God to cover us with the shadow of His wings (Ps. 17:8).

How wonderful that our gracious Father has provided a shield to shelter us from every evil. For example, our text will help to prevent us from falling into the evil of unorthodox doctrines, for we are in danger of misinterpreting Scripture to make God say what He does not. If we depart from the teaching of the Holy Spirit, we are in danger of distorting the letter of the Word and losing its spirit, and of deriving from the letter a meaning that can ruin our souls.

How can we escape this? Peter, speaking by the Holy Spirit, pointed out our safeguard in the words of our text: *"But grow in grace, and in the knowledge of our Lord and Saviour Jesus Christ. To him be glory both now and for ever. Amen."* While you search the Scriptures and become acquainted with them, see to it that you *"grow in grace."* While you desire to learn and understand doctrine, long, above all, to grow in *"the knowledge of our Lord and Saviour Jesus Christ."*

However, let both your study of Scripture, and your growth in grace and in the knowledge of Christ, still be subservient to a higher object: that you may live to bring *"glory both now and for ever"* to Him who has loved you and has bought you with His blood. Let your heart forever say *"Amen"* to this doxology of praise. In this way, you will be kept from all destructive errors, and you will not *"fall from your own stedfastness"* (2 Pet. 3:17).

It appears, then, that our text is a heavenly remedy for certain diseases to which even students of Scripture are exposed.

We see in our text two "trumpets." One is blown from heaven to earth: *"Grow in grace, and in the knowledge of our Lord and Saviour Jesus Christ."* The other sounds from earth to heaven: *"To him be glory both now and for ever."* Another way to look at our text is to divide it into two matters. First, there is a matter of theology: *"Grow in grace."* Second, there is a matter of doxology: *"To him be glory both now and for ever."* A third way to look at our text, and the way that we will look at it in this chapter, is this: first, we have a divine command with a special direction; and second, a grateful doxology with a significant conclusion.

GROWING IN GRACE

I will begin at the beginning. We have here a divine command with a special direction: *"Grow in grace, and in the knowledge of our Lord and Saviour Jesus Christ."*

Who Can Grow in Grace?

"Grow in grace." What does this mean? We see in the very beginning of this verse that it was written to those who have been awakened by grace. This

verse does not apply to the unsaved at all. Dead things cannot grow. Those who are alive unto God by the resurrection of Jesus Christ are the only ones who have any power or ability to grow. The great Life-giver must first implant the seeds of life, and then afterward, those seeds can germinate and grow. Therefore, this text does not apply to you who are *"dead in trespasses and sins"* (Eph. 2:1). You cannot grow in grace, because you are still under the curse of the law, and the wrath of God remains on you (John 3:36). Tremble, repent, believe; and may God have mercy on you.

However, if you are alive from the dead, if you have been awakened by the Spirit of God who is now in you, you are instructed to grow, for growth will prove that you are spiritually alive. A post planted in the earth does not grow, but a tree rooted there increases from a sapling to a forest king. Drop a pebble into the richest soil, and many years from now, it will still be a pebble of the same size. However, plant a seed, and it will sprout and develop.

Growing in Every Virtue

You who are alive unto God, see to it that you grow in all the graces. Grow in your roots—that is, in your faith. Seek to believe God's promises better than you do now. From that trembling faith that says, *"Lord, I believe; help thou mine unbelief"* (Mark 9:24), grow upward to the faith that *"stagger[s] not at the promise of God"* (Rom. 4:20). Like Abraham, believe that *"what he [has] promised, he [is] able also to perform"* (v. 21). Let your faith increase in extent; believe more truth. Let it increase in constancy; do not allow it to be feeble or wavering, always tossed about with every wind of false doctrine (Eph. 4:14). Let your faith daily increase in simplicity, resting more fully on the finished work of your Lord Jesus Christ.

In addition to faith, see to it that your love also grows. If your love has been a spark, pray that the spark may become an all-consuming flame. If you have brought to Christ only a little, pray that you may bring your all. Pray that you may offer your all in such a way that, like Mary's broken alabaster box, the King Himself may be satisfied with the perfume (Matt. 26:7–13). Ask that your love may become more extended—that you may have love for all the saints. Ask that it may be more practical, that it may move your every thought, every word, and every deed. Ask that it may be more intense, that you may become like a burning and shining light whose flame is love for God and man.

In addition to love, pray that you may grow in hope. Along those lines, pray that *"the eyes of your understanding being enlightened...ye may know what is the hope of his calling, and what* [are] *the riches of the glory of his inheritance in the saints"* (Eph. 1:18). Pray that you will continually look *"for that blessed hope, and the glorious appearing of the great God and our Saviour Jesus Christ"* (Titus 2:13). Pray that the hope not yet realized may enable you to wait patiently (Rom. 8:25). Pray that you may, by hope, enter into the joys of heaven while you are on earth. Pray that hope may give you immortality while you are still mortal, may give you resurrection before you die, may allow you to see God clearly where otherwise you could see only a dim reflection.

Ask that you may grow in humility, until you can say, "[I] *am less than the least of all saints*" (Eph. 3:8). Ask that you may grow in consecration, until you can cry, *"For to me to live is Christ, and to die is gain"* (Phil. 1:21). Ask that you may grow in contentment, until you can say, *"I have learned, in whatsoever state I am, therewith to be content"* (Phil. 4:11). Advance in likeness to the Lord Jesus, so that your very enemies may notice that you have been with Jesus and have learned from Him (Acts 4:13). In short, if there is any virtue, if there is anything that is praiseworthy, if there is anything that is lovely and of good report (Phil. 4:8), if there is anything that can increase your usefulness, that can add to your happiness, that can make you more useful to man and more glorious toward God, grow in it. Growth is necessary, for we have not *"already attained,"* nor are we *"already perfect"* (Phil. 3:12).

As a Tree Grows

I want to remind you, faithful believer in Christ, that the Bible compares you to a tree—a tree of the Lord's planting (Isa. 61:3). Seek to grow as a tree grows. Pray that this year you may grow downward, that you may know more of your own vileness, more of your own nothingness, and so be rooted in humility. Pray that your roots may penetrate below the mere topsoil of truth into the great rocks that underlie the uppermost layer, so that you may grasp the doctrines of eternal love, God's unchangeable faithfulness, complete satisfaction, union with Christ, and the eternal purpose of God. These deep things of God will yield a rich and abundant sap, and your roots will drink from the hidden fountains of *"the deep that lieth under"* (Gen. 49:25).

This growth of your roots will be a growth that will not add to your fame or your vanity, but it will be invaluable during the storms of life. It will be a growth the value of which no heart can conceive when the hurricane is tearing up the hypocrite and hurling into the sea of destruction the *"trees whose fruit withere*[d], *without fruit, twice dead, plucked up by the roots"* (Jude 12).

As you root downward, seek to grow upward. Send out the top shoot of your love toward heaven. The trees send out their spring shoots and their midsummer shoots. You can see, at the top of the fir tree, that new green child of spring—the fresh shoot that lifts its hand toward the sun. In the same way, you should also long for more love and greater desires for God, a closer communion with Him in prayer, a sweeter spirit of adoption as His child, a more intense and intimate fellowship with the Father and with His Son Jesus Christ. This act of mounting upward will add to your beauty and to your delight.

In addition, pray to grow on either side. Stretch out your branches. Let the shadow of your holy influence extend as far as God has given you opportunities. But see to it also that you grow in fruitfulness, for to increase the bough without adding to the fruit is to diminish the beauty of the tree. Labor this year, by God's grace, to bring forth more fruit for Him than you have ever done. Lord, give to each reader more of the fruits of penitence for sin, faith in the great sacrifice of Jesus, love for the Savior, and zeal for the conversion of souls. We do not want to be like the gleanings of the vintage, when there is only here and there a cluster on the uppermost bough. We want to be like the valley of Eshcol in the Promised Land (Deut. 1:24–25), whose presses burst with new wine.

This is what it means to grow in grace: to root downward, to shoot upward, to extend your influence like far-reaching branches, and to bring forth fruit for the Lord's glory.

As a Child Grows

I will borrow another comparison from Scripture. Fellow believer, we are not only compared to trees, but to children. Let us grow as babes do, nourished by unadulterated milk (1 Pet. 2:2). Like babes, let us grow steadily, slowly, but surely and certainly. In this way, we will grow a little each day, but much through the years. Oh, that we may grow in strength as a child does, until the little, wobbling limbs of our faith are firm, muscular legs—the legs of a young man who runs without weariness. May we have untiring feet—the feet of a strong man who walks without fainting. (See Isaiah 40:31.) So far, our wings are unfledged, and we can hardly leave the nest. Lord, command our growth to proceed until we can mount as with the wings of eagles toward You, surmounting clouds and storms, and dwelling in the serene presence of the Most High. Let us develop all our powers. Let us ask that we may no longer be little infants, but that many inches may be added to our height until we become mature in Christ Jesus.

Let us especially pray that we may grow as healthy children—uniformly. Beloved, it is a bad sign if a child's head enlarges but not the rest of his body, or if his arm or foot is swollen disproportionately. Beauty consists in every part having the correct proportion. A vigorous judgment should not be yoked with a cold heart, nor a clear eye with a withered hand. A giant's head looks odd on a dwarf's shoulders. A virtue nourished at the expense of others is like a fattened cannibal fed on the flesh and blood of its murdered relatives; it is not fitting for a Christian to harbor such a monster. Let us pray that faith and love and every grace may be developed, that not one power may be left unnurtured or ungrown. Only in this way can we truly *"grow in grace, and in the knowledge of our Lord and Saviour Jesus Christ."*

Reasons to Grow in Grace

Do you ask why we should grow in grace? Let us say, beloved, that if we do not advance in grace, it is a sorrowful sign. It is a mark of unhealthiness. It is a sickly child who does not grow, an unhealthy tree that sends forth no fresh shoots. Furthermore, it may be a sign not only of unhealthiness but of deformity. If a man's shoulders have grown to a certain breadth, but his lower limbs refuse to lift him to a proportionate height, we call him a dwarf, and we somewhat pity him because he is malformed. O Lord, let us grow, for we do not want to be ill-formed. We want to be children like God our Father; we want to be pleasing in appearance, every one of us like the sons of a king.

Not to grow may be, moreover, the sign of death. Our lack of growth may say to us, "To the extent that you do not grow, you do not live." If you are not increasing in faith, love, and grace; if you are not ripening for the harvest, fear and tremble. Perhaps you have only a reputation for being alive while you are actually destitute of life (Rev. 3:1). Perhaps you are a painted counterfeit—a lovely picture of a flower, drawn by the artist's skillful hand, but lacking life, lacking the power that makes the flowers germinate, blossom, and bring forth fruit. Advance in grace, because not to progress foretells many evil things and might indicate the worst of all things: lack of spiritual life.

Grow in grace, because, beloved, to increase in grace is the only pathway to lasting nobility. Oh, don't you wish to stand with that noble host who have served their Master well and have entered into their eternal rest? Who does not wish to have his name written with the great missionaries—with Judson and with Carey, with Williams and with Moffat? What Christian has no ambition to find his name written among those servants of God—Whitefield, Grimshaw, Newton, Romaine, Toplady, and others who preached the Word with power? Do you wish to go back to the vile dust from where we sprung up, unwept, unhonored, and unsung? If so, then remain as you are; stop marching forward. Littleness and lowness lie at your door; be small and ignoble, if you desire. But if you want to be a prince in God's Israel, if you want to be a mighty warrior for the Cross of Christ, then pray this prayer: "Lord, help me grow in grace, so that I may be a faithful servant and receive Your commendation in the end."

To grow is not only to be noble; it is to be happy. The man who stops growing refuses to be blessed. With most businessmen, if they do not win, they lose. With the warrior, if he does not gain in the battle, his enemy is getting an advantage. The wise man who gets no wiser grows more foolish. The Christian who does not learn more about his Lord and become more like Him, knows less about his Lord and becomes less like Him. If our armor is unused, it will tarnish. If our arms are not strengthened by effort, they will be weakened by laziness. Our happiness declines as our spirituality fades.

To be happy, I say, we must go forward. Ahead is sunlight. Ahead is victory. Ahead is heaven. Ahead is Christ! To stand still is danger; no, it is death. O Lord, for the sake of our happiness, help us to advance; for the sake of our usefulness, let us ascend. Oh, if only we would grow in grace, if only we would grow stronger in faith, mightier in prayer, more fervent in heart, holier in life, who can tell how much we might accomplish? Men who walk lightly leave faint footprints, but men who have the tread of Roman soldiers stamp their footprints on the sands of time, never to be erased. Let us live in such a way that, in our own time and in the future, the world may be better and Christ's church more prosperous for our having lived. For this reason, if for no other, let us grow in grace.

Oh, I want to fire you with holy ambition today! If I could snatch from some ancient altar a live coal such as that which fell on the lips of Isaiah, I would say to you, *"'Lo, this hath touched thy lips'* (Isa. 6:7). Go forth in the spirit and power of God, even the Most High, and live as those who did not count their lives dear unto themselves (Acts 20:24) so that they could serve their Master and *'be found in him'* (Phil. 3:9). I point you to the redeemed who have entered *'within the veil'* (Heb. 6:19) and who rest in eternal glory, and I say that they won the victory by grace, and growth in grace was the means of their triumph. Imitate them. Press forward as they did, and through grace you also will inherit their rest and their triumph, and will sit down with them forever."

Ways to Grow in Grace

Do you ask *how* you will grow in grace? The answer is simple. The One who gave you grace must give you more of it. Where you first received grace, there you must receive the increase of that grace. The One who made the cattle and created man is the same One who afterward said, *"Be fruitful, and multiply, and replenish the earth"* (Gen. 1:28). So the One who has given you grace must speak in your heart with His omnipotent decree, and say to that grace, *"'Be fruitful, and multiply, and replenish'* the soul until its inherent emptiness is filled, until the natural desert rejoices and blossoms like a rose (Isa. 35:1)."

At the same time, you should use all the spiritual means available, and those means are much prayer, a more diligent search of the sacred Scriptures, a more constant fellowship with the Lord Jesus Christ, greater activity in His cause, a devout reception of all revealed truth, and so forth. If you do these things, you will never be dwarfed or stunted in your growth, for the One who has given you life will thus enable you to fulfill the word that He spoke to you by His apostle: *"Grow in grace, and in the knowledge of our Lord and Saviour Jesus Christ."*

GROWING IN KNOWLEDGE

I have explained the divine exhortation of our text. However, notice that our text also contains a special direction: *"And in the knowledge of our Lord and Saviour Jesus Christ."*

My fellow believer in the Lord Jesus, we must see to it that we ripen in the knowledge of Him. Oh, that we may know more of Him in His divine nature and in His human relationship to us. Oh, that we may know more of Him in His finished work, in His death, in His resurrection, in His present glorious intercession, and in His future royal advent. To know more of Christ in His work is, I think, a blessed means of enabling us to work more for Christ.

We also must study in order to know more of Christ in His character—in that divine combination of perfection, faith, zeal, deference to His Father's will, courage, meekness, and love. He was the Lion of the tribe of Judah, yet the Man on whom the dove descended in the waters of baptism. Let us thirst to know Him of whom even His enemies said, *"Never man spake like this man"* (John 7:46), and of whom His unrighteous judge said, *"I find no fault in him"* (John 19:4).

Above all, let us long to know Christ in His person. Endeavor to become better acquainted with the Crucified One. Study His hands and His feet. Stay close to the Cross. Let the sponge, the vinegar, and the nails be subjects of your devout attention. Seek to penetrate into His very heart. Search those deep, far-reaching caverns of His undiscovered love, that love that can never find a rival and can never know a parallel. If you can add to this a knowledge of His sufferings, you will do well. Oh, if you can grow in the knowledge of fellowship, if you drink of His cup and are baptized with His baptism, if you abide in Him and He in you, you will be blessed. This is the only growth in grace that is true growth. All growth that does not lead us to increase in the knowledge of Christ is only the puffing up of the flesh and not the building up of the Spirit.

Grow in the knowledge of Christ, then. And do you ask why? Oh, if you have ever known Him, you will not ask that question. He who does not long to know more about Christ, knows nothing about Him yet. Anyone who has ever sipped this new wine will thirst for more, for although Christ satisfies, it is such a satisfaction that we want to taste more and more and more. Oh, if you know the love of Jesus, I am sure that *"as the hart panteth after the water brooks"* (Ps. 42:1), so you will pant after Him. If you say you do not desire to know Him better, then I tell you that you do not love Him, for love always cries, "Nearer, nearer,

nearer." To be absent from Christ is hell, but to be present with Christ is heaven. As we get nearer to Him, our heaven becomes more heavenly, and we enjoy it more and feel more that it is of God.

Oh, may you come to the very well of Bethlehem, and not merely to receive a pitcherful from it, as David did, at the risk of the lives of three mighty men (1 Chron. 11:17–19). May you come to the well and drink—drink from the well itself, from that bottomless wellspring of eternal love. Oh, may the secret of the Lord be with you, and may you be in the secret place of the Most High! My Master, if you would permit me to ask You one thing as a special favor, it would be this, that I may *"know him, and the power of his resurrection...being made conformable unto his death"* (Phil. 3:10). Nearer to You, blessed Lord, nearer to You; this is my cry! The Lord grant that our cry may be heard, that we may grow in the knowledge of Christ!

We wish to know Christ as our Lord—Lord of every thought and every desire, of every word and every act. We want to know Him as our Savior, too, our Savior from every indwelling sin, our Savior from every past evil deed, our Savior from every future trial. All hail Jesus! We salute You as Lord. Teach us to feel Your kingship over us, and to feel it every hour. All hail the Crucified One! We acknowledge You as Savior. Help us to rejoice in Your salvation and to feel the plenitude of that salvation in all and every part of spirit, soul, and body, being wholly saved by You.

Beloved, may you *"grow in grace, and in the knowledge of our Lord and Saviour Jesus Christ."*

PRAISING THE LORD

In the second part of the text, we have a grateful thanksgiving with a significant conclusion: *"To him be glory both now and for ever. Amen."*

The apostles, I must remark, very frequently suspended their writing in order to lift up their hearts in praise. Praise is never out of season. It is no interruption to interrupt any task in order to praise and magnify our God. *"To him be glory."*

Let every heart joyously feel this doxology. *"To him,"* the God who made the heavens and the earth, without whom *"was not any thing made"* (John 1:3). *"To him"* who in His infinite compassion became the surety of the covenant. *"To him"* who became a baby. *"To him"* who was *"despised and rejected of men; a man of sorrows, and acquainted with grief"* (Isa. 53:3). *"To him"* who on the bloody tree poured out His heart's life so that He could redeem His people. *"To him"* who said, *"I thirst"* (John 19:28), and, *"It is finished"* (v. 30). *"To him"* whose lifeless body slumbered in the grave. *"To him be glory."*

"To him" who burst the bonds of death. *"To him"* who *"ascended up on high, [and] led captivity captive"* (Eph. 4:8). *"To him"* who sits at the right hand of the Father and who will soon come to be our Judge. *"To him be glory both now and for ever."*

Yes, *"to him,"* you atheists, who deny Him. *"To him,"* you kings who vaunt your splendor and will not have this Man to reign over you (Luke 19:14). *"To him,"* you people who stand up against Him, and you rulers who take counsel against Him (Ps. 2:2). *"To him"*—the King whom God has set on His holy hill of Zion (v. 6)—*"to him be glory."*

"To him be glory" as the King of Kings and Lord of Lords. *"Wonderful, Counsellor, the mighty God, the everlasting Father, the Prince of Peace"* (Isa. 9:6). Again, *"hosanna in the highest"* (Matt. 21:9)! Hallelujah! King of Kings and Lord of Lords! *"To him be glory"* as Lord. *"To him be glory"* as Savior. He alone has redeemed us unto God by His blood. He alone has *"trodden the winepress"* (Isa. 63:3); He has come *"from Edom, with dyed garments from Bozrah… glorious in his apparel, travelling in the greatness of his strength"* (v. 1). *"To him be glory."*

Hear it, you angels: *"To him be glory."* Clap your wings. Cry, "Hallelujah! *'To him be glory.'"* Hear it, you *"spirits of just men made perfect"* (Heb. 12:23). Play the strings of your celestial harps and say, "Hallelujah! Glory to Him who has redeemed us unto God by His own blood." *"To him be glory."* Church of God, respond! Let every godly heart say, *"To him be glory."* Yes, *"to him be glory,"* you fiends of hell, as you tremble at His presence and see the key of your prison swinging on His belt. Let heaven and earth and hell, let things that are and were and will be, cry, *"To him be glory."*

The apostle added, *"Now." "To him be glory… now."* Oh, beloved, do not postpone the day of His triumph; do not put off the hour of His coronation. Now, now.

> Bring forth the royal diadem,
> And crown Him Lord of all.

"To him be glory...now," for now, today, God *"hath raised us up together, and made us sit together in heavenly places in Christ Jesus"* (Eph. 2:6). *"Beloved, now are we the sons of God"* (1 John 3:2). Now our sins are forgiven; now we are clothed in His righteousness. Now our feet are on a rock, and our steps are established (Ps. 40:2). Who would defer the time of singing hosannas? *"To him be glory... now."* Oh, seraphim above, *"To him be glory...now,"* for you continually cry, *"Holy, holy, holy, is the LORD of hosts"* (Isa. 6:3). Adore Him yet again, for, *"To him be glory...now."*

Notice the last part of the doxology: *"And for ever."* Never will we cease our praise. Time, you will grow old and die. Eternity, your unnumbered years will speed their everlasting course. But forever, forever, forever, *"to him be glory."* Is He not a *"priest for ever after the order of Melchizedek"* (Ps. 110:4)? *"To him be glory."* Is He not King forever—King of Kings and Lord of Lords, the Everlasting Father? *"To him be glory...for ever."*

Never will His praises cease. That which was bought with blood deserves to last as long as immortality endures. The glory of the Cross must never be eclipsed. The luster of the grave and of the Resurrection must never be dimmed. Oh, my beloved, my spirit begins to feel the ardor of the immortals. I anticipate the songs of heaven. My tongue, if it only had celestial liberty, would begin even now to join in those "melodious sonnets sung by flaming tongues above." O Jesus, You will be praised forever. As long as immortal spirits live, as long as the Father's throne endures, forever, forever, forever, unto You be glory.

SAYING AMEN

Now, there is a very significant conclusion to this verse: *"Amen."* Beloved, I want to work this amen out—not as a matter of doctrine, but as a matter of blessed ecstasy. Join your heart with mine in affirming this doxology. *"To him be glory both now and for ever. Amen."*

By the way, the Puritans pointed out—and it is a very remarkable thing—that under the old law, there was no amen to the blessings; the only amen was to the curses. When they pronounced the curses, all the people said amen. (See Deuteronomy 27:9–26.) Under the old law, there was never an amen to the blessings.

Now, it is an equally remarkable and more blessed thing that under the Gospel there is no amen to the curses; the only amen is to the blessings. For example, 2 Corinthians 13:14 says, *"The grace of the Lord Jesus Christ, and the love of God, and the communion of the Holy Ghost, be with you all. Amen."* On the other hand, 1 Corinthians 16:22 says, *"If any man love not the Lord Jesus Christ, let him be Anathema* [accursed]." No amen. There is no amen to the curse under the Gospel, but *"all the promises of God in him* [Christ] *are yea, and in him Amen"* (2 Cor. 1:20).

Our Hearts' Desire

What does this amen in our text mean? *Amen* has four meanings in Scripture. First, it is the desire of the heart. Jesus said, *"Surely I come quickly"*

(Rev. 22:20). The apostle John responded, *"Amen. Even so, come, Lord Jesus"* (v. 20). We say amen at the end of a prayer to signify, "Lord, let it be so"—it is our hearts' desire.

Now, beloved, join your heart with mine, then, for it is all a heart matter here. *"To him be glory both now and for ever. Amen."* Is that your heart's desire? If not, you cannot say amen to it. Does your heart long, pant, thirst, groan, and cry out after Christ, so that you can say, every time you bend your knee in prayer, *"Thy kingdom come. Thy will be done in earth, as it is in heaven....For thine is the kingdom, and the power, and the glory, for ever. Amen"* (Matt. 6:10, 13)? Can you say, "Amen, Lord, let Your kingdom come"? Beloved, if you can say it in this sense, if it is your heart's desire that Christ's glory be extended and that His kingdom come, say amen. My heart glows with this amen. The Judge of all knows how my heart longs to see Jesus magnified.

> Amen, with joy divine, let earth's
> Unnumber'd myriads cry;
> Amen, with joy divine, let heaven's
> Unnumber'd choirs reply.

Our Hearts' Belief

However, the word *amen* signifies more than this; it means the affirmation of our faith. We only say amen to that which we really believe to be true. We add our affidavit, as it were, to God's promise, affirming that we believe Him to be faithful and true. Do you have any doubts that Jesus Christ is glorious now and will be forever? Do you doubt His being glorified by angels, cherubim, and seraphim today? Don't you believe, my beloved, that *"they that dwell in the wilderness shall bow before him; and his enemies shall lick the dust"* (Ps. 72:9)? If you do believe this, if you have faith today amid the world's obstinacy and the sinner's pride, amid abounding superstition and dominant evil, if you still have faith to believe that Christ will be glorious forever and ever, then say amen. *"To him be glory both now and for ever. Amen."*

There are more who can desire these things than there are who believe them. Nevertheless, God remains faithful.

> This little seed from heaven
> Shall soon become a tree;
> This ever blessed leaven
> Diffused abroad must be:
> Till God the Son shall come again,
> It must go on. Amen! Amen.

Our Hearts' Joy

There is yet a third meaning to this amen. It often expresses the joy of the heart. When in ancient times they crowned a Jewish king, the high priest took a horn of oil and poured it on his head. Then came forward a herald, and the moment he sounded the trumpet, someone said in a loud voice, "God save the king! God save the king!" and all the people said amen, and one shout went up to heaven. With joyful hearts, they welcomed the king; they hoped that he would be a prosperous ruler whom God would use to bless them and make them victorious.

Now, as you see King Jesus sitting on Mount Zion with death and hell underneath His feet, as today you anticipate the glory of His advent, as today you are expecting the time when you will reign with Him forever and ever, doesn't your heart say amen?

In a season of my life in which I was in great darkness of mind and weakness of body, I remember one text that encouraged me beyond all measure. There was nothing in the text about me; it was no promise to me, but it was something about Christ. It was this:

> *God also hath highly exalted him, and given him a name which is above every name: that at the name of Jesus every knee should bow, of things in heaven, and things in earth, and things under the earth.* (Phil. 2:9–10)

Oh, it seemed so joyous that He was exalted! What did it matter what became of me? What did it matter what became of all believers? King Jesus is worth ten thousand of us. Let our names perish, but let His name last forever. Beloved, I bring forth the King to you. I bring Him before the eyes of your faith today. I proclaim Him King again. If you desire Him to be King and if you rejoice in His reign, say amen. Crown Him! Crown Him! *"To him be glory both now and for ever."* Joyous heart, lift up your voice and say amen.

Yea, amen, let all adore Thee,
　High on Thine exalted throne!
Savior, take Thy power and glory;
　Claim the kingdoms for Thine own:
　　O come quickly!
　Hallelujah! Come, Lord, come.

Our Hearts' Resolution

Lastly, this is a very solemn truth: amen is sometimes used in Scripture as an amen of resolution. It means, "I, in the name of God, solemnly pledge myself that in His strength I will seek to make it so; *'to him be glory both now and for ever.'*"

Last week I walked through the long galleries that vanity has dedicated to all the glories of France. I passed through room after room, where especially I saw the triumphs of Napoleon. Surely, as you walk through the pages of Scripture, you walk through a much more marvelous picture gallery, in which you see the glories of Christ. This Book contains the memorials of His honors.

In another place in Paris, there stands a column made with the cannons taken by the Emperor in battle. A mighty trophy, certainly. O Jesus, you have a better trophy than this—a trophy made of souls forgiven; of eyes that wept, but whose tears have been wiped away; of broken hearts that have been healed; and of saved souls that rejoice evermore. What wonderful trophies Christ has to make Him glorious, *"both now and for ever"*—trophies of living hearts that love Him; trophies of immortal spirits who find their heaven in gazing upon His beauties!

What glories will be Christ's forever when you and I and all the millions upon millions He has bought with His blood are in heaven! Oh, when we have been there thousands of years, we will feel as fresh an ecstasy as when we first came there. If our spirits should be sent on any errand and we have to leave our Master's presence for a moment, oh, with what wings of a dove we will fly back to behold His face again! When we all surround that throne, what songs will come forth from these lips of mine, the chief of sinners saved by blood! What hymns you will give Him, you who have had your iniquities cleansed and are saved today! What praise all those multitudes who have been partakers of His grace will give Him!

But this has more to do with *"for ever."* What do you say about our glorifying Him *"now"*? Oh, beloved, do make this your prayer today: "Lord, help me to glorify You. I am poor; help me to glorify You by contentment. I am sick; help me to give You honor by patience. I have talents; help me to extol You by using them for You. I have time, Lord; help me to redeem it, so that I may serve You. I have a heart to feel, Lord; let that heart feel no love but Yours and glow with no flame but affection for You. I have a head to think, Lord; help me to think of You. You have put me in this world for something, Lord; show me what it is, and help me to work out my life's purpose, for I do desire to say amen. I cannot do much; my amen is only a weak one. Yet, as the widow put in her two mites, which was all she had to live on, so, Lord, I put my time and eternity into Your treasury. It is all Yours. Take it, and thus I say amen to Peter's doxology."

And now, will you say amen to this? I pray that you will do so. You who do not love Christ cannot say amen. Remember that you are under the law. There is an amen for all the curses to you; there is none for the blessings while you are under the law. Oh, poor sinner under the law, may this be the day when your slavery under the law will come to an end! "How can this be?" you ask. By faith in Christ. *"He that believeth on him is not condemned"* (John 3:18). Oh, believe on Him, and then your joyful heart will say amen. Then you will say, "Loudest of all the saints in heaven, I will shout amen when I see the royal crown brought forth, and Jesus is acknowledged Lord of all."

I trust that as long as I live it may be mine to give my amen to that doxology: *"To him be glory both now and for ever. Amen."*

Chapter 4

The Joy of the Lord

The joy of the LORD is your strength.
—Nehemiah 8:10

And the singers sang loud, with Jezrahiah their
overseer. Also that day they offered great sacrifices,
and rejoiced: for God had made them rejoice with great
joy: the wives also and the children rejoiced: so that
the joy of Jerusalem was heard even afar off.
—Nehemiah 12:42–43

I would like to consider with you the subject of
joy. Perhaps as we think about joy and remark
on the many reasons for its existence, some of
those reasons may operate on our hearts, and we
may lay this book down as recipients of tremendous
joy. I will consider this a beneficial book if it causes
the people of God to rejoice in the Lord, and especially
if those who have been weighed down and burdened
in their souls will receive the oil of joy in exchange for
their mourning (Isa. 61:3). It is a significant thing to

comfort the Lord's mourners. It is a work especially dear to the Spirit of God, and it is, therefore, not to be taken lightly.

Holy sorrow is precious before God and is not a hindrance to godly joy. Carefully note, in connection with our first text, Nehemiah 8:10, that the fact that there is great mourning is no reason why there should not soon be great joy, for the very people who were told by Nehemiah and Ezra to rejoice were, at the time, weeping for their sins. *"For all the people wept, when they heard the words of the law"* (v. 9). The vast congregation that had gathered before the water gate to hear the teaching of Ezra was awakened and cut to the heart. The people felt the edge of God's law like a sword opening up their hearts—tearing, cutting, and killing. They had good reason to cry. But as they were crying, it was time to let them feel the Gospel's balm and hear the Gospel's music; therefore, Nehemiah and Ezra changed their tune and consoled them, saying,

> *This day is holy unto the LORD your God; mourn not, nor weep....Go your way, eat the fat, and drink the sweet, and send portions unto them for whom nothing is prepared: for this day is holy unto our Lord: neither be ye sorry; for the joy of the LORD is your strength.*
> *(Neh. 8:9–10)*

Now that they were penitent and had sincerely turned to their God, they were told to rejoice. Even as certain fabrics need to be dampened before they will absorb the bright colors with which they are to be dyed, so our spirits need the rain of repentance before they can receive the radiant coloring of delight. The glad news of the Gospel can only be printed on wet paper. Have you ever seen the world around you shine more than after a rain shower? Then the sun transforms the raindrops into gems, the flowers look up with fresher smiles and glitter with the droplets of their refreshing bath, and the birds among the dripping branches sing with notes more rapturous because they have paused awhile. In the same way, when the soul has been saturated with the rain of penitence, the clear shining of forgiving love makes the flowers of gladness blossom all around.

The steps by which we ascend to the palace of delight are usually moistened with tears. In *The Pilgrim's Progress,* by John Bunyan, grief for sin is the porch of the House Beautiful, in which the guests are full of the joy of the Lord. I hope, then, that the mourners who read this book will discover and enjoy the meaning of that divine blessing in the Sermon on the Mount: *"Blessed are they that mourn: for they shall be comforted"* (Matt. 5:4).

From our texts, I will draw several themes for consideration. First, there is a joy of divine origin— *"the joy of the LORD."* Second, that joy is a source of strength for all who share in it—*"the joy of the LORD is your strength."* Third, I will show that such strength always reveals itself practically—our second text will help us there. I will close this chapter by noticing, in the fourth place, that this joy, and, consequently, this strength, are within our reach today.

OUR JOY COMES FROM THE LORD

First, there is a joy of divine origin. Since the source of this joy is the Lord, it will necessarily be a high and sublime joy. From the time that man fell in the Garden, he has too often sought enjoyment where the Serpent finds his. God said to the Serpent, *"Upon thy belly shalt thou go, and dust shalt thou eat all the days of thy life"* (Gen. 3:14). This was the Serpent's doom, and man, with foolish ambition, has tried to find his delight in his sensual appetites. Man has tried to content his soul with earth's poor dust. But the joys of time cannot satisfy an undying nature. Once a soul is awakened by the eternal Spirit, it cannot fill itself with worldly pleasure. It cannot even fill itself with the common delights of this life. To try to do so would be like trying to store up wind and eat it for breakfast.

However, beloved, we do not have to search for joy. It is brought to us by the love of God our Father—joy refined and satisfying, suitable for immortal spirits. God has not left us to wander among those unsatisfactory things that mock the chase that they invite. No, He has given us appetites that carnal things cannot content, and He has provided suitable satisfaction for those appetites. He has stored up at His right hand pleasures forevermore (Ps. 16:11), which even now He reveals by His Spirit to those chosen ones whom He has taught to long for them.

In the pages that follow, let us endeavor to analyze that special pleasure that our text calls *"the joy of the LORD."*

The Joy of the Lord

The Source and Object of Our Joy

First, our joy springs from God and has God for its object. The believer who is in a spiritually healthy state rejoices mainly in God Himself. He is happy because there is a God, and because God, in His person and character, is what He is. All the attributes of God become continual sources of joy to the thoughtful, contemplative believer, for such a person says within his soul, "All these attributes of my God are mine. His power is my protection. His wisdom is my guidance. His faithfulness is my foundation. His grace is my salvation."

He is a God who cannot lie, who is faithful and true to His promise. He is all love, and, at the same time, infinitely just and supremely holy. Why, to one who knows that this God is his God forever and ever, the contemplation of God is enough to make the eyes overflow with tears because of the deep, mysterious, unspeakable bliss that fills the heart.

There was nothing in the character of Jupiter, or any of the false gods of the heathen, to make a pure and holy spirit glad. But there is everything in the character of Jehovah both to purify the heart and to thrill it with delight. How wonderful it is to think about all the Lord has done, how He has revealed Himself since long ago, and especially how He has displayed His glory in the covenant of grace and in the person of the Lord Jesus Christ. How precious is the thought that He has revealed Himself to me personally and has caused me to see Him as my Father, my Friend, my Helper, my God.

Oh, if there is one phrase from heaven that cannot be excelled, even by the brightness of heaven itself, it is this phrase: "My God, my Father," along with that precious promise: *"I will be to them a God, and they shall be to me a people"* (Heb. 8:10). There is no richer comfort to be found. Even the Spirit of God can reveal nothing more delightful to the Christian's heart. How marvelous it is when the child of God admires God's character and marvels at His acts and at the same time thinks, "He is my God. I have taken Him to be mine, and He has taken me to be His. He has grasped me with the hand of His powerful love. Having loved me with an everlasting love, with lovingkindness He has drawn me to Himself (Jer. 31:3). My Beloved is mine, and I am His (Song 6:3)." Why, then his soul would gladly dance like David before the ark of the Lord, rejoicing in the Lord with all its might (2 Sam. 6:14).

Reconciliation, Acceptance, and Adoption

The Christian who is living near to God finds a further source of joy in a deep sense of reconciliation to God, of acceptance with God, and yet, beyond that, of adoption and close relationship to God. Doesn't it make a person glad to know that his sins, which had once provoked the Lord, are all blotted out and that not one of them remains? Isn't he delighted to know that though he was once alienated from God, and far away from Him because of his wicked works, he is brought near by the blood of Christ? The Lord is no longer an angry Judge pursuing him with a drawn sword, but a loving Father with whom he can share his sorrows and find comfort for every heartfelt grief.

Oh, to know, beloved, that God actually loves us! I have often said I cannot preach on that theme, for it is a subject to muse on in silence, a matter to sit and meditate on for hours. The fact that the Infinite loves an insignificant creature, a fleeting moth, a declining shadow—isn't this amazing? That God pities me I can understand. That God reaches down and has mercy on me I can comprehend. But for Him to love me, for the pure to love a sinner, for the infinitely great to love a worm, is matchless, a miracle of miracles! Such thoughts do indeed comfort the soul.

Then add to this the fact that divine love has brought us believers into actual relationship with God, so that we are His sons and daughters—this again is a river of sacred pleasure. *"Unto which of the angels said he at any time, Thou art my Son?"* (Heb. 1:5). No angel, no ministering spirit, though perfect in obedience, has received the honor of adoption. To us, even to us frail creatures of the dust, is given a gift denied to Gabriel. Through Jesus Christ the Firstborn, we are members of the family of God! Oh, the depths of joy that lie in being God's child and Christ's joint-heir! Words are useless here.

The joy springing from the Spirit of adoption is very much a portion of the believer's bliss. He cannot be an unhappy man who can cry, *"Abba, Father"* (Rom. 8:15). The Spirit of adoption is always attended by love, joy, and peace, which are fruits of the Spirit, for we have not received the spirit of bondage again to fear, but we have received the Spirit of liberty and joy in Christ Jesus (v. 15). "My God, my Father"—oh, how sweet the sound.

71

You may be thinking, "But all of God's people do not experience this joy." Sad to say, I agree, but I also add that it is their own fault. It is the right of every believer to live in the assurance that he is reconciled to God, that God loves him, and that he is God's child. If he does not live this way, he has only himself to blame. If there is any starving at God's table, it is because the guest cheats himself, for the feast is superabundant. If, however, a believer begins to consistently live with a sense of pardon through the sprinkling of the precious blood, and with a delightful sense of perfect reconciliation with the great God, he will possess a joy unspeakable and full of glory (1 Pet. 1:8). I pray that you will begin to live this way.

Fearlessness about the Future

But, beloved, this is not all. The joy of the Lord in our spirits springs also from an assurance that our entire future, regardless of what may happen, is guaranteed by divine goodness. We are joyful when we know that, as children of God, the love of God toward us never changes. The believer feels complete satisfaction in leaving himself in the hands of eternal and unchangeable love.

However happy I may be today, if I am in doubt about tomorrow, there is a worm at the root of my peace. Although the past may now be pleasant in retrospect, and the present satisfying and enjoyable, if the future looks gloomy and frightening, my joy is shallow. If my salvation is still a matter of chance and uncertainty, unmingled joy is not mine, and deep peace is still out of my reach. But my outlook changes when I know that He in whom I have rested has enough power and grace to complete what He has begun in me and for me (Phil. 1:6). I see my future differently when I see the work of Christ as no halfway redemption, but a complete and eternal salvation. Peace comes when I perceive that the promises are established on an unchangeable basis, and are *"yea"* and *"Amen"* (2 Cor. 1:20) in Christ Jesus, confirmed by oath and sealed by blood. When I realize all this, my soul has perfect contentment.

It is true that as I look forward I may see long avenues of tribulation, but glory is at the end of them. Battles may be foreseen, and woe to the believer who does not expect them, but the eye of faith perceives the crown of victory. Deep waters appear on the maps of our journeys, but faith can see Jehovah fording these rivers with us, and she anticipates the day when we will ascend the banks of the nearby shore and enter into Jehovah's rest.

When we have received these priceless truths into our souls, we are satisfied with God's grace and are full of the goodness of the Lord. There is a theology that denies believers this comfort. I will not enter into controversy over it, but I sorrowfully hint that those who believe the errors of that doctrinal system will be heavily punished by losing the comfort that the truth would have brought into their souls. For my part, I value the Gospel not only for what it has done for me in the past, but for the guarantee that it gives me of eternal salvation. *"I give unto* [my sheep] *eternal life; and they shall never perish, neither shall any man pluck them out of my hand"* (John 10:28).

Close Fellowship with God

Now, beloved, I have not yet taken you into the great depths of joy, though these streams are certainly by no means shallow. However, there is a deepness of delight for every Christian when he comes into actual fellowship with God. I spoke of the truth that God loves us, and the fact that we are related to Him by ties most near and dear. But, oh, when these doctrines become experiences, then we are indeed anointed with the oil of gladness. When we enter into the love of God, and it enters into us, when we walk with God consistently, then our joy is like the Jordan River at harvesttime, when it overflows all its banks.

Do you know what it means to walk with God and to experience the joy that Enoch had? Do you know what it means to sit at Jesus' feet and to experience the joy that Mary had? Do you know what it means to lean your head on Jesus' chest and to experience the joy that John had? Oh, yes, communion with the Lord is not a matter of mere words with some of us. We have known it in the midst of affliction. We have known it in the solitude of many a night of interrupted rest. We have known it when experiencing discouragements and sorrows and defamations, and all sorts of problems. And we know that one teaspoon of fellowship with Christ is enough to sweeten an ocean of tribulation. Only to know that He is near us, and to see the sparkle in His dear eyes, would transform even hell itself into heaven, if it were possible for us to enjoy His presence there.

However, you do not and cannot know this bliss, you who spend your time greedily consuming alcohol. You do not know what this bliss means—you have not dreamed of it, nor could you comprehend it even if someone were to tell you about it. As the beast in the field does not know the far-reaching thoughts of the One who reads the stars and threads the spheres in the heavens, so the carnal man cannot even imagine the joys that God has prepared for those who love Him (1 Cor. 2:9). But any day and every day, when our hearts seek to know them, He reveals them to us by His Spirit (v. 10).

This is *"the joy of the LORD"*—fellowship with the Father and with His Son Jesus Christ. Beloved, if we reach this point, we must work to maintain our standing, for our Lord says to us, *"Abide in me"* (John 15:4). The habit of communion is the life of happiness.

The Privilege of Serving Christ

Another form of *"the joy of the LORD"* will visit us in a practical way every day; it is the honor of being allowed to serve Him. It is a joy worth worlds to be allowed to do good. To teach a little child the alphabet in Christ's name will give a true heart a taste of the joy of the Lord, if it is consciously done for the Lord's sake alone. To give a meal to the hungry, to visit the sick, to comfort the mourner, to aid the poor, to instruct the ignorant—any and all of such Christian works, if done in Jesus' name, will, in their measure, clothe us in Jehovah's joy.

Moreover, happy are we if, when we cannot work, we are enabled to lie still and suffer, for submission is another silver pipe through which the joy of the Lord will come to us. It is satisfying to smart beneath God's rod and to feel that, if God would have us suffer, it is happiness to do so. It is precious to fall back with the faintness of our nature, but at the same time with the strength of God's grace, and say, *"Thy will be done"* (Matt. 6:10). It is joy, when we are crushed like an olive, to yield nothing but the oil of thankfulness. It is delight, when bruised beneath the flail of tribulation, to lose nothing but the chaff, and to yield to God the precious grain of entire submissiveness. Why, this is a little heaven on earth. To exult in tribulations also is equal to more than a few steps of ascent toward the likeness of our Lord.

Perhaps the usual times of communion that we have with our Beloved, though exceedingly precious, will never equal those that we enjoy when we have to break through thorns and briers to be with Him. When we follow Him into the wilderness, then we feel that the love of our marriage to Christ is doubly sweet (Jer. 2:2). It is a joyous thing when, in the midst of mournful circumstances, we still feel that we cannot mourn because the Bridegroom is with us. Blessed is that believer who, in the most terrible storm, is not driven away from his God, but instead rides nearer to heaven on the crest of the enormous waves. Such happiness is the Christian's lot.

I am not saying that every Christian possesses such happiness, but I am sure that every Christian ought to. There is a highway to heaven, and all on it are safe. But in the middle of that road there is a special way, an inner path, and all who walk on it are happy as well as safe. Many professing Christians are barely on the right path; they walk in the ditch by the roadside. Because they are safe there, they are content to put up with all the inconveniences of their walk. But the believer who walks in the very center of the road that God has constructed will find that no lion will be there, nor will any ferocious beast go up on it. There the Lord Himself will be his companion and will manifest Himself to him.

You shallow Christians whose faith in Christ is barely alive, whose Bibles are unread, whose prayer times are few, whose communion with God is a thing of inconsistency—you do not have the joy of the Lord, nor are you strong. I implore you, do not rest as you are, but let your weakness motivate you to seek the means of strength. That means of strength is to be found in a pleasant medicine, as sweet as it is profitable—the delicious and effective medicine of *"the joy of the LORD."*

MEDITATING ON GOD BRINGS JOY AND STRENGTH

Too many pages would be required for me to fully share my remarks on this very fruitful subject. Therefore, I will turn to my second topic, which I began to explain in the previous section: this joy is a source of great strength.

Very briefly let us consider this thought. Joy is a source of strength because joy arises from meditations that always strengthen the soul. Much of the depth of our godliness will depend on our contemplativeness. Many people, after receiving a doctrine, put it on the shelf. They are orthodox, they have received the truth, and they are content to keep that truth on hand as dead weight. Reader, how can you be benefited if you store your granary with wheat but never grind the wheat for bread, or sow it in the furrows of your fields? He is a joyful Christian who uses the doctrines of the Gospel for spiritual meat, as they were meant to be used.

Why, some people might as well have an unorthodox creed instead of an orthodox one for all the difference that it makes to them. Having the notion that they know the truth, and imagining that simply knowing it is sufficient, they do not consider, contemplate, or regard the truths that they profess to believe. Consequently, they derive no benefit from them.

Now, to contemplate the great truths of divine election, eternal love, justification by faith through the blood of Christ, and the indwelling and perpetual abiding of the Holy Spirit in His people—to think over these thoughts—is to extract joy from them, and doing so also strengthens the mind. To press the heavenly grapes by meditation, and make the red wine flow forth in torrents, is an exercise as strengthening as it is exhilarating. Joy comes from the same truths that support our strength, and it comes by the process of meditation.

Again, *"the joy of the LORD"* within us is always the sign and symbol of strong spiritual life. Holy joyfulness is evidence of spiritual vigor. I said earlier that he who has spiritual joy has gained it by communion with God, but communion with God is also the surest fosterer of strength. You cannot be with a strong God without getting strength yourself, for God is always a transforming God. As we regard and look upon Him, we change until we become, in our measure, like our God.

The warmth of southern France, which perhaps you have heard a little bit about, does not come from soft, balmy winds. No, it comes from the sun, for at sunset, the temperature falls. Also, in Italy, you might be on one side of the street and think it is May, and then cross the street into the shade and find it as cold as January. The sun makes all the difference.

Even so, a man who walks in the sunlight of God's countenance is warm and strong for that very reason. The sunlight of joy usually goes with the warmth of spiritual life. As the light of joy varies, so does the warmth of holy strength. He who dwells in the light of God is both happy and strong. He who goes into the shade and loses the joy of the Lord becomes weak at the same time. In this way, the joy of the Lord becomes our strength because it is an indicator of its rise or fall. When a soul is really vigorous and active, it is like a torrent that dashes down the mountainside, scorning to be bound by frost in wintertime. In just a few hours of cold weather, the stagnant pools and slowly moving streams are enchained in ice; but the snow king must bring forth all his strength before he can restrain the rushing torrent. So, when a soul dashes on with the sacred force of faith, it is hard to freeze it into misery. Its vigor secures its joy.

Strength for Suffering and Service

Furthermore, the believer who possesses *"the joy of the LORD"* finds it his strength in another respect:

it fortifies him against temptation. What is there that he can be tempted with? He already has more than the world could ever give him as a reward for treachery. He is already rich; who can entice him with the wages of unrighteousness? He is already satisfied; who can seduce him with pleasing baits? He simply says, *"Should such a man as I flee?"* (Neh. 6:11).

The rejoicing Christian is equally fortified against persecution. Someone who wins at the rate that a joyful believer wins can well afford to be laughed at. "You may scoff," he says, "but I know within my soul what true faith is, and your scoffing will not make me relinquish the pearl of great price." Moreover, such a person is made strong to bear affliction, for all the sufferings put on him are only a few drops of bitterness flung into his cup of bliss, to give a deeper tone to the sweetness that absorbs them.

Such a believer also becomes strong for service. What can a person who is happy in his God not do? By his God he leaps over a wall, or breaks through a troop (2 Sam. 22:30). He is strong, too, for any kind of self-sacrifice. To the God who gives him all and is his perpetual portion, the joyful believer gives up all that he has and does not think of it as a sacrifice. He is simply storing his treasure in his own special treasure-house—the God of his salvation.

Portrait of a Strong Christian

A joyous Christian, such as I am now picturing in my mind's eye, is strong in a calm, restful manner.

Regardless of what happens, he is not upset or disturbed. He is not afraid of bad news; his heart is steadfast, trusting in the Lord (Ps. 112:7). The fretful person, on the other hand, is always weak. He is in a hurry and does things poorly. In contrast, the joy-filled believer is quiet; he bides his time and is full of strength. Such a believer, though he is humble, is firm and steadfast. He is not carried away with every wind, or blown over by every breeze (Eph. 4:14). He knows what he knows, and believes what he believes. The golden anchor of his hope enters within the veil and holds him tightly (Heb. 6:19). His strength is not feigned—it is real.

The happiness that comes from communion with God does not cause him to be boastful. He does not talk of what he can do, but he simply does it. He does not say what he could endure, but he endures all that comes. He himself does not always know what he can do; his weakness is more apparent to him because of the strength that the Holy Spirit puts in him. But when the time comes, his weakness only illustrates the divine might within him, while he goes calmly on, conquering and to conquer.

His inner light makes him independent of the outward sun. His secret granaries make him independent of the outward harvest. His inner fountains keep him safe from dread, even though the brook Cherith may dry up. (See 1 Kings 17:1–9.) He is independent of men and angels, and fearless of devils. Everyone may turn against him if they please, but since God Himself is his exceeding joy, he will not miss their love or mourn their hate. He stands where others fall. He sings where others weep. He wins where others flee. He glorifies his God where others bring dishonor on themselves and on the sacred name. God grant us the inner joy that arises from real strength, and is so linked with it that it is partly its cause.

JOY BRINGS RESULTS

But now I must go on to notice that this joy and this strength lead to practical results. Please read our second text again, Nehemiah 12:42–43:

> *And the singers sang loud, with Jezrahiah their overseer. Also that day they offered great sacrifices, and rejoiced: for God had made them rejoice with great joy: the wives also and the children rejoiced: so that the joy of Jerusalem was heard even afar off.*

In these verses, we observe some of the fruits of holy joy and godly strength.

Enthusiastic Praise

First, strength and joy lead to great praise. *"The singers sang loud"*; their singing was hearty and enthusiastic. Sacred song is not a minor matter. Someone once said, "Praying's the end of preaching." Couldn't we go further and say, "Praising's the end of praying"? After all, preaching and praying are not the chief end of man; it is the glorifying of God, of which praising God vocally is one form. Preaching is sowing, prayer is watering, but praise is the harvest.

God aims at His own glory, and so should we. The Lord says, *"Whoso offereth praise glorifieth me"* (Ps. 50:23). Be diligent then to sing His praises with understanding.

It is shocking to me to be present in places of worship where not a tenth of the people ever venture to sing at all, and these do it through their teeth so very softly that one needs to have a special hearing aid to enable him to hear the dying strain. Out with such mumbling and murdering of the praises of God! If people's hearts were joyous and strong, they would scorn such miserable worship.

Let us be glad when we come together and unite in singing. Let us all sing to the Lord. Let us not rely on musical instruments to do our praising for us. The human voice is the greatest musical instrument that exists, by far. There is certainly no melody or harmony like those created by living tongues. Let us not rely on a choir or paid musicians to praise for us. God wants to hear the voices of all of His people united in praise.

Couldn't our churches have more praise services? In the church that I pastor, we have had a praise meeting every now and then. Shouldn't our churches hold praise meetings every week? Shouldn't prayer meetings be made more joyous than ever by praise? The singing of God's people should be—and if they were more full of divine strength it would be—more constant and universal. How sinners chant pagan praises in the streets! Some of us can hardly rest in the middle of the night without crude sounds of revelry startling us. Should the worshipers of wine sing so enthusiastically, and we be silent? We are not often guilty of disturbing the world with our music. The days in which Christian zeal interfered with the wicked seem to have gone by. We have settled down into more orderliness, and I am afraid into more lukewarmness as well. Oh, to be free to shout our praises!

Beloved, wake up your singing again. May the Lord help us to sing to Him more, and make us all to praise Him with heart and with voice, until even our adversaries say, "The Lord has done great things for them," and we reply, "Yes, you speak the truth. *'The LORD hath done great things for us; whereof we are glad'* (Ps. 126:3)."

Perhaps there has not been great blessing on our churches because they have not given God the thanksgiving of which He is worthy. During all the times in which we are in trouble, we are anxious and prayerful. When the leader of our country is sick, news of his progress is issued every hour or so. But, oh, when God's mercy comes, very little news is put out to call on us to bless and praise the name of God for His mercies. Let us praise the Lord *"from the rising of the sun unto the going down of the same"* (Ps. 113:3). *"For great is the LORD, and greatly to be praised"* (1 Chron. 16:25).

Great Sacrifices

The next result of strength and joy is great sacrifice. *"That day they offered great sacrifices, and rejoiced."* What day does the church of God now set aside to make great sacrifices? I have not seen it on the calendar lately. Unfortunately, if people make any sacrifice, they very often do so in a way that indicates that they would avoid making it if they could. Few make great sacrifices and rejoice. You can persuade a person to give a considerable amount of money; a great many arguments overcome him at last, and he gives because he would be ashamed not to. But in his heart, he wishes you had not come that way but had gone to some other donor.

The most acceptable gift given to God is the gift given joyfully. It is wonderful to feel that whatever good your gift may do for the church or the poor or the sick, it is twice as beneficial to you to give it. It is good to give because you love to give, even like the flower that pours forth its perfume because it never dreamed of doing otherwise; or like the bird that quivers with song because it is a bird and finds pleasure in its notes; or like the sun that shines, not by constraint, but because, being a sun, it must shine; or like the waves of the sea that flash back the brilliance of the sun because it is their nature to reflect and not to hoard the light.

Oh, to have such grace in our hearts that we joyfully make sacrifices to our God! May the Lord grant that we may have much of this grace, for the bringing of the tithes into the storehouse is the way to blessing, as the Scripture says:

> *Bring ye all the tithes into the storehouse, that there may be meat in mine house, and prove me now herewith, saith the LORD of hosts, if I will not open you the windows of heaven, and pour you out a blessing, that there shall not be room enough to receive it.*　　　*(Mal. 3:10)*

Happiness in Everyday Life

They *"rejoiced: for God had made them rejoice with great joy."* Singing and giving are not the only signs of the joy of God's people. In addition to these, other expressions of joy are sure to follow. When the wheels of a machine are well oiled, the whole machine runs easily; and when a man has the oil of joy, then in his business, and in his family, he glides along smoothly and harmoniously because he is a happy man.

On the other hand, there are some professing Christians who imagine that the sorrow of the Lord is their strength. They glory in the spirit of bondage and in an unbelieving experience, having great acquaintance—too much acquaintance—with the corruption of their hearts. They try to say that believers' deformities are their beauty, and their faults are their virtues. Such men denounce all who rejoice in the Lord; they tolerate only the unbelieving. Their strength lies in being able to take you through all the catacombs of nature's darkness, and to show you the rottenness of their evil hearts.

Well, let those who want to have such strength have it, but I am persuaded that our text is closer to wisdom: *"The joy of the LORD is your strength."* While we know a little about our corruption and mourn over it, while we know a little about the world's troubles and sometimes lament as we bear them, there is a joy in the perfect work of Christ, and a joy in our union with Him, that lifts us far above all other considerations. God becomes to us such a strength that we cannot help showing our joy in our ordinary lives.

Joy Shared with Family and Friends

The text also tells us that holy joy leads to family happiness. *"The wives also and the children rejoiced."* It is so in my own church. I have lately noticed several households that God has blessed, and I have rejoiced to see that father and mother know the Lord, and that even the youngest of the family has been brought to Jesus. Oh, households are happy indeed when the joy is not confined to one person but all partake of it. I greatly dislike that Christianity that makes a person feel, "My only concern is that *I* make it to heaven." Why, a person concerned only about himself is like a furnace that heats itself but does not heat the house.

Too many need all the religion they can get to encourage their own hearts, and their poor families and neighbors sit shivering in the cold of ungodliness. Do not be like that. Be like those well-built furnaces that send out all the heat into the house. Send out the heat of godliness into your house, and let all the neighbors participate in the blessing, for our text finishes with, *"The joy of Jerusalem was heard even afar off."* The joy of the Lord should be observed throughout our neighborhoods, and many who might otherwise have been indifferent to true religion will then ask, "What makes these people glad and creates such happy households?" In this way, your joy will be God's missionary.

YOU CAN HAVE JOY AND STRENGTH

This joy and this strength are both within our reach! *"For God had made them rejoice with great joy.*" God alone can give us this great joy. It is within the reach of anyone, for God can give it to one as well as to another. If it depended on our good works or our natural abilities, we could never reach it. But if God is the source and giver of it, He may give it to me as well as to you, and to you as well as to someone else.

According to our texts, what were the conditions under which God gave this joy? Well, first, He gave it to these people because they were attentive hearers (Neh. 8:3). They were not passive hearers, but they listened intently as the Word was read. As it was read to them, they absorbed it, receiving it into their souls. An attentive hearer is on his way to being a joyous receiver.

Having heard the Word, they felt the power of it, and they wept (v. 9). Does that seem like the way to joy? No, but it was. They received the threats of the Law, with all their terrors, into their souls. They allowed the hammer of the Word to break them in pieces. They submitted themselves to the words of reproof. Oh, that God would incline you to do the same thing, for this, again, is the way in which God gives joy. The Word is heard; the Word is felt.

After they had felt the power of the Word, we see that they worshiped God devoutly (v. 6). They bowed their heads. Their postures indicated what they felt within. Worshipers who truly adore God with penitent hearts will never complain of boring Sundays. Adoration helps to bring us into joy. He who can bow low enough before the throne will be lifted as high before that throne as his heart can desire.

We read also that these hearers and worshipers understood clearly what they heard (v. 8). Never be content with hearing a sermon unless you can understand it. If there is a truth that is above you, strain after it; strive to know it. Bible reader, do not be content with going through the words of a chapter of Scripture. Ask the Holy Spirit to tell you the meaning, and use the proper means for finding out that meaning. Ask those who know, and use your own enlightened judgment to discover the meaning.

When will we be done with formalism in worship and come into living adoration? Sometimes, for all the true singing that there is, the song might as well be in Latin or in Greek. Oh, to know what we are singing, to know what we are saying in prayer, to know what we are reading, to get at it, to come right into it, to understand it—this is the way to holy joy.

I need to make one other point. These people, when they had understood what they had devoutly heard, were eager to obey (Neh. 8:14–17). They obeyed not only the common points of the Law that had been observed and demonstrated by former generations of Israelites, but they discovered an old institution that had been buried and forgotten. It did not matter to them that it had not been observed for a long time. God had commanded it, and they celebrated it, and in so doing, a special joy came to them.

Oh, for the time when all believers will search the Word of God, when they will not be content with saying, "I have joined myself with a certain body of believers. They do such and such; therefore, I do the same." May no one say to himself any longer, "This is the rule of my church," but may each of us say, "I am God's servant, not the servant of man, not the servant of man-made rules and regulations, not the servant of the prayer book or the catechism. To my own Master I stand (Rom. 14:4), and the only law book I acknowledge is the book of His Word, inspired by His Spirit." Oh, it will be a blessed day, when every person will say, "I want to know what I am wrong about. I desire to know what I am supposed to do. I am eager to follow the Lord fully." If your joy in God leads you to practical obedience, you may rest assured that it has made you strong in the very best manner.

May we be a strong people, and consequently a joyous people, in the strength and joy of the Lord. May sinners in great numbers look unto Jesus and be saved.

Chapter 5

The Same Yesterday, Today, and Forever

Jesus Christ the same yesterday,
and to day, and for ever.
—Hebrews 13:8

I have written on this text before, but I do not need to be at all afraid of writing on the same text twice. God's Word is inexhaustible. It may be trodden in the winepress many times and still generously yield wine. We should not hesitate to write a second time from the same passage, any more than anyone going to a well would be ashamed to put down the same bucket twice, or any more than anyone would feel at all distressed about sailing down the same river twice. There is always a freshness about gospel truth. Although the subject matter may be the same, there are ways of putting it in fresh light in order to bring new joy to those who meditate on it.

Is it unnecessary for me to repeat my teachings concerning Christ? Is it useless for you to read over and over again the same things about the King? No, we can afford to give and receive the same teachings again. Repetitions concerning Jesus are better than varieties on any other subject. As the French monarch declared that he would sooner hear the repetitions of Louis Bourdaloue, the famous French Jesuit, than the novelties of another, we may declare the same concerning our Lord Jesus. We would sooner hear again and again the precious truths that glorify Him than listen to the most eloquent orations on any other theme in all the world.

There are a few works of art and wonders of creation that you could gaze upon every day of your life and yet not tire of them. Everyone who has ever looked at the ocean or at Niagara Falls knows that, look as often as you may, though you see precisely the same object, there are new tints, new motions of the waves, and new flashes of light that forbid the least bit of monotony and that give to the waters an ever enduring charm. This is the way it is with that sea of all delights that is found in the dear Lover of our souls.

Thus, we come to the old subject of this old text, and may the blessed Spirit give us new anointing while we meditate on it. We will see that our text provides us with three main themes. First, note our Lord's personal name: Jesus Christ. Second, notice His memorable attribute: He is *"the same yesterday, and to day, and for ever."* Third, examine His claims, which are derived from the possession of such a character.

THE PERSONAL NAMES OF OUR LORD

Jesus

"Jesus" is the first name for our Lord that is
mentioned in the text. That is our Lord's Hebrew
name, "Joshua," or *"Jesus."* The word signifies a
Savior: *"Thou shalt call his name JESUS: for he shall
save his people from their sins"* (Matt. 1:21). The
name was given to Him while He was still in His
cradle.

> Cold on His cradle the dewdrops are shining;
>> Low lies His head with the beasts of the stall;
> Angels adore Him, in slumber reclining,
>> Maker, and Monarch, and Savior of all.

While He was still an infant feeding at His
mother's breast, He was recognized as Savior, for
the fact of God's becoming incarnate was the pledge,
guarantee, and commencement of human salvation.
At the very thought of His birth, the Virgin sang,
"My spirit hath rejoiced in God my Saviour" (Luke
1:47). There was hope that man would be lifted up to
God when God came down to man. Jesus in the
manger deserved to be called the Savior, for when it
can be said that *"the tabernacle of God is with men,
and he...dwell*[s] *with them"* (Rev. 21:3), there is
hope that all good things will be given to the fallen
race.

He was called Jesus in His childhood—the holy
child Jesus. It was as Jesus that He went up with
His parents to the temple and sat down with the

teachers, hearing them and asking them questions. Yes, Jesus, as He taught the very first principles of His doctrine, was a Savior, liberating the minds of men from superstition and setting them loose from the traditions of their ancestors. Even as a child, He scattered the seeds of truth, the elements of a glorious liberty that would emancipate the human mind from the iron bondage of false philosophy and ritualism.

It was so evident in His active life that Jesus was the Savior that He was commonly called by that name by both His friends and foes. It was as Jesus the Savior that He healed the sick, raised the dead, delivered Peter from sinking, and rescued from shipwreck the ship tossed on the Sea of Galilee. In all the teachings of His midlife, in those laborious three years of diligent service, both in His public ministry and in His private prayer, He was still Jesus the Savior; for by His active, as well as by His passive obedience, we are saved. All during His earthly life, He made it clear that the Son of Man had come *"to seek and to save that which was lost"* (Luke 19:10). If His blood redeems us from the guilt of sin, His life shows us how to overcome its power. If by His death upon the cross He crushed Satan for us, by His life of holiness He teaches us how to break the Dragon's head within us.

He was the Savior as a babe, the Savior as a child, the Savior as the toiling, laboring, tempted man. But He was most clearly Jesus the Savior when dying on the cross. Even Pilate called Him *"Jesus,"* or Savior, when he wrote His title on the cross, which read, *"JESUS OF NAZARETH THE KING OF THE*

JEWS" (John 19:19). When Pilate was asked to change this title, he said, *"What I have written I have written"* (v. 22).

Preeminently on the cross, He was the Savior, being made a curse for us so that *"we might be made the righteousness of God in him"* (2 Cor. 5:21). In fact, it was after beholding the dying agonies of his Master that the Beloved Apostle wrote, *"We have seen and do testify that the Father sent the Son to be the Saviour of the world"* (1 John 4:14). At Calvary, it was remarked that the Son of Man *"saved others"* (Matt. 27:42), but, through blessed incapacity prompted by love, *"himself he* [could not] *save"* (v. 42). When He was made to feel the wrath of God on account of sin, and pains unknown were suffered by Him as our Substitute, when He was made to pass through the thick darkness and burning heat of divine wrath, then He was, according to Scripture, *"the Saviour of all men, specially of those that believe"* (1 Tim. 4:10).

Yes, it was on the cross that Christ was especially a Savior. If He were nothing better than our example, how unfortunate we would be! We might be grateful for the example if we could imitate it, but without the pardon that spares us, without the grace that gives us power for holiness, the brightest example would only increase our grief. To be shown a picture of what we ought to be, without being given a method to attain that standard, would only mock our misery. But Jesus first pulls us out of the horrible pit into which we are fallen, taking us out of the mud and mire by the power of His atoning sacrifice. Then, having set our feet on a rock by virtue of His merits, He Himself leads the way onward to perfection. Therefore, He is a Savior both in life and in death.

> That Jesus saves from sin and hell,
>   Is truth divinely sure;
> And on this rock our faith may rest
>   Immovably secure.

Still bearing the name of Jesus, our Lord rose from the dead. Evangelists delight in calling Him Jesus when they speak of His appearance to Mary Magdalene in the garden or His appearance to the disciples when they were gathered together behind locked doors. When He is spoken of as the Risen One, He is always spoken of as Jesus the Savior. Beloved, since we are justified by His resurrection, it is fitting that we regard Him as Savior when speaking of His resurrection. Salvation is strongly linked with a risen Christ, because we see Him, by His resurrection, destroying death, breaking down the prison of the tomb, carrying away, like another Samson, the gates of the grave. He is our Savior because He has already vanquished the enemy that will be the last to be completely destroyed—Death. He rose so that we, having been saved from sin by His death, can be saved from death through His resurrection.

Jesus is the title by which He is called in glory, for *"him hath God exalted with his right hand to be a Prince and a Saviour, for to give repentance to Israel, and forgiveness of sins"* (Acts 5:31). He is today *"the saviour of the body"* (Eph. 5:23). We adore Him as *"the only wise God our Saviour"* (Jude 25). *"He is able also to save them to the uttermost that come unto*

*God by him, seeing he ever liveth to make interces-
sion for them"* (Heb. 7:25). As Jesus, He will come
again, and we are *"looking for that blessed hope, and
the glorious appearing of the great God and our Saviour Jesus Christ"* (Titus 2:13). Our daily cry is,
"Even so, come, Lord Jesus" (Rev. 22:20).

Yes, Jesus is the name by which He is known in
heaven at this hour. By the name of Jesus, the angel
spoke of Him before He was conceived by the Virgin.
By the name of Jesus, the angels serve Him and do
His bidding, for He said to John on Patmos, *"I Jesus
have sent mine angel to testify unto you these things"*
(Rev. 22:16). The angels prophesied His second
coming using that sacred name. They came to Jesus'
followers who stood looking up into heaven after His
ascension, and they said, *"Ye men of Galilee, why
stand ye gazing up into heaven? this same Jesus,
which is taken up from you into heaven, shall so
come in like manner as ye have seen him go into
heaven"* (Acts 1:11). Under this name, the devils fear
Him, for didn't an evil spirit say, *"Jesus I know, and
Paul I know; but who are ye"* (Acts 19:15)?

The name of Jesus is the spell that binds the
hearts of cherubim in chains of love, and it is the
name that makes the hosts of hell tremble and
cower. This name is both the joy of the church on
earth and the joy of the church above. It is a household name for our dear Redeemer among the family
of God below, and up there they still sing it.

> Jesus, the Lord, their harps employs:
>   Jesus, my Love, they sing!
> Jesus, the life of both our joys,
>   Sounds sweet from every string.

The Meaning of "Jesus"

Henry Craik of Bristol, a man of God, wrote a little book on the study of the Hebrew language. In it, he used the word *Jesus* as an example of how much may be gathered from a single Hebrew word, for the name of Jesus is particularly rich and meaningful to the mind of the Hebrew scholar. Its root word means "amplitude, spaciousness." It later came to mean "setting at large, setting free, delivering." Then it came to mean what it commonly means today, namely, "Savior."

There are actually two words in the name *Jesus*. The one is a contraction of the word *Jehovah;* the other is the word that I have just now explained to you as ultimately coming to mean "salvation." Broken down to its simplest terms, the word *Jesus* means "Jehovah–Salvation." The first part of His name declares the glorious essence and nature of Christ as Jehovah, *"I AM THAT I AM"* (Exod. 3:14). The second part of His name reveals His great work for us in setting us free and delivering us from all distress.

Think, beloved believer, of the amplitude, the spaciousness, the breadth, the abundance, the boundless all-sufficiency laid up in the person of the Lord Jesus. *"It pleased the Father that in him should all fulness dwell"* (Col. 1:19). You do not have a limited Christ; you do not have a narrow Savior. Oh, the infinity of His love, the abundance of His grace, the exceeding greatness of the riches of His love toward us! There are no words in any language that can sufficiently describe the unlimited, infinite extent of the riches of the glory of Christ Jesus our Lord.

The word that lies at the root of this name *Jesus,* or *Joshua,* sometimes has the meaning of riches, and who can tell what a wealth of grace and glory is laid up in our Emmanuel? According to Henry Craik, another form of the same word signifies "a cry." The psalmist said, *"Hearken unto the voice of my cry, my King, and my God"* (Ps. 5:2). Thus, salvation, riches, and a cry are all derived from the same root, and all are found in our "Joshua," or Christ. When His people cry out from their prisons, then He comes and sets them free. He comes with all the fullness and wealth of His eternal grace, with all the plenitude of His overflowing power. Delivering His people from every form of bondage, He enables them to enjoy the riches of the glory treasured up in Himself.

If this interpretation makes the name of Jesus a little bit more dear to you, I greatly rejoice. Just think, if there is so much wealth stored up in His name, what must be stored up in His very self! And, if we can honestly say that it would be difficult to give the full meaning of this one Hebrew name that belongs to Christ, how much more difficult would it be to give the full meaning of all His character? If His name alone is such a mine of excellence, what must His person be? If His name, which is only a part of Him, smells so sweetly of myrrh, aloes, and cassia (Ps. 45:8), oh, what must His blessed person be but *"a bundle of myrrh"* (Song 1:13) that we will forever wear around our necks to be the perfume of our lives and the delight of our souls?

Precious is the name of Jesus,
Who can half its worth unfold?

99

Far beyond angelic praises,
  Sweetly sung to harps of gold.

Precious when to Calvary groaning,
  He sustain'd the cursed tree;
Precious when His death atoning,
  Made an end of sin for me.

Precious when the bloody scourges
  Caused the sacred drops to roll;
Precious when of wrath the surges
  Overwhelm'd His holy soul.

Precious in His death victorious,
  He the host of hell o'erthrows;
In His resurrection glorious,
  Victor crowned o'er all His foes.

Precious, Lord! beyond expressing,
  Are Thy beauties all divine;
Glory, honor, power, and blessing,
  Be henceforth forever Thine.

Christ

I have written about the Hebrew name of God's Son. Now let us reverently consider the second title given to Him in our text—*"Christ."* That is a Greek name, a Gentile name, meaning "anointed." In our text, we have the Hebrew name *Joshua,* or *Jesus,* then the Greek name *Christos,* or *Christ,* so that we may see that there is no longer Jew or Gentile, but that all are one in Jesus Christ (Gal. 3:28). The word *Christ*, as I have mentioned, means "anointed," and as such, our Lord is sometimes called *"the Christ"* (Matt. 16:16), or *"the very Christ"* (John 7:26). At other times, He is called *"the Lord's Christ"* (Luke 2:26), and sometimes *"the Christ of God"* (Luke 9:20). He is the Lord's Anointed, our King, and our Shield.

This word *Christ* teaches us three great truths. First, it indicates His offices. He exercises offices in which anointing is necessary; there are three of them: the office of king, the office of priest, and the office of prophet.

Christ is King in Zion, anointed *"with the oil of gladness above* [His] *fellows"* (Ps. 45:7), even as it was said long ago,

> I have found David my servant; with my holy
> oil have I anointed him: with whom my hand
> shall be established: mine arm also shall
> strengthen him....I will set his hand also in
> the sea, and his right hand in the riv-
> ers....Also I will make him my firstborn,
> higher than the kings of the earth.
>
> *(Ps. 89:20–21, 25, 27)*

Saul, the first king of Israel, was anointed with only a vial of oil, but David was anointed with a horn of oil, as if to signify his greater power and his greater kingdom. But as for our Lord Jesus Christ, He has received the Spirit of anointing without measure (John 3:34). He is the Lord's Anointed, for whom an unquenchable lamp is ordained. The Scripture says, *"There will I make the horn of David to bud: I have ordained a lamp for mine anointed"* (Ps. 132:17).

Beloved, as we think about the name *Christ,* let us reverently yield our souls up to the One whom God has anointed to be King. Let us stand up for His rights over His church, for He is King of Zion, and none have a right to rule there except under and in subjection to the great Head over all, who in all things will have the preeminence (Col. 1:18). Let us stand up for His rights within our own hearts, seeking to thrust out anything that competes with Him for our affection, desiring to keep our souls chaste for Christ. Let us make every member of our bodies, though previously they might have surrendered themselves to sin, become subservient to the anointed King who has a right to rule over them.

Next, the Lord Christ is Priest. Priests had to be anointed. Israelites were not supposed to take this office upon themselves, nor could they become priests without going through the ceremony that set them apart. Jesus Christ our Lord has had grace given to Him that no priest ever had. The outward anointing of the priest was only symbolical, while His anointing was true and real. He has received what their oil only portrayed in type and shadow; He has the real anointing from the Most High.

Beloved, let us always look at Christ as the anointed Priest. My friend, you can never come to God except through the ever living and truly anointed High Priest of your faith's profession. Oh, never for a moment seek to come to God without Him, or through any pretender who may call himself a priest. High Priest of the house of God, we see You thus ordained, and we give our cause into Your hands. Offer our sacrifices for us; present our prayers. Take our praises, put them into the golden censer (Rev. 8:3), and offer them Yourself before Your Father's throne. Rejoice, beloved, every time you hear the name *Christ,* knowing that He who wears it is anointed to be Priest.

Regarding the prophetic office, the Scriptures reveal that Elisha was anointed to prophesy, and likewise Jesus Christ is the Prophet anointed among His people. Peter told Cornelius of *"how God anointed Jesus of Nazareth with the Holy Ghost and with power: who went about doing good, and healing all that were oppressed of the devil; for God was with him"* (Acts 10:38). He was anointed to preach the Good News and to sit as Master in Israel. We should consider no man's teaching to be authoritative except the testimony of the Christ. The teaching of Christ is our creed, and nothing else.

I thank God that in my church we do not have to divide our allegiance between some venerable set of articles and the teaching of our Lord. We have one Master, and we do not acknowledge the right of any man to bind another's conscience. Even if a man is great in piety and deep in learning, like Augustine and Calvin, whose names we honor, for God honored them, still he has no dominance over the private judgment of God's people. Jesus Christ is the Prophet of Christendom. His words must always be the first and the last appeal.

This, then, is the meaning of the word *Christos*: He is anointed as King, Priest, and Prophet. But it means more than that. The name *Christ* declares His right to those offices. He is not King because He sets Himself up as such. God has set Him up as King upon His holy hill of Zion and has anointed Him to rule. He is also Priest, but He has not taken the priesthood upon Himself, for He is the atoning sacrifice that God has set forth for human sin. The Lord God has appointed Christ to be the mediator; He has chosen Christ to be the only mediator between God and man. And as for His prophesying, Christ does not speak on His own; on the contrary, He has revealed to us the things that He has learned from the Father. He does not come as a prophet who assumes office; God has anointed Him to preach the Good News to the poor and to come among His people with the welcome news of eternal love.

Moreover, this anointing signifies a third thing. Even as He has the office, and as it is His by right, so He has the qualifications for the work. He is anointed to be King. God has given Him royal power, wisdom, and government; He has made Him fit to rule in the church and to reign over the world. There is no better king than Christ—none as majestic as He who wore the crown of thorns—for He will one day wear the crown of universal monarchy.

He has the qualifications of a priest, too—qualifications that even Melchizedek did not have (Heb. 7:1–3, 15–17), qualifications that cannot be found in the long lineage of the house of Aaron. Blessed Son of God, You are perfect in Yourself, and You do not need a sacrifice for Your own sake. Yet, You have presented unto God an offering that has perfected forever those whom You have set apart (Heb. 10:14). Now, You do not need to make a further offering. You have forever put away sin.

It is the same way with our Lord's prophesying; He has the power to teach. *"Grace is poured into thy lips: therefore God hath blessed thee for ever"* (Ps. 45:2). All the words of Christ are wisdom and truth. The substance of true philosophy and sure knowledge is to be found in the One who is the wisdom and the power of God (1 Cor. 1:24).

Oh, that word *Christ!* It seems to grow on us as we think it over. It shows us the offices of Christ, His right to those offices, and His qualifications for them.

> Christ, to Thee our spirits bow!
>> Prophet, Priest, and King art Thou!
> Christ, anointed of the Lord,
>> Evermore be Thou adored.

Now, put the two titles together and ring out the harmony of the two melodious notes: Jesus Christ—Anointed Savior! Oh, how blessed! Don't you see that our Beloved is a Savior appropriately appointed, a Savior abundantly qualified? My friends, if God has appointed Christ to be the Savior of sinners, why do you question His decision? God presented Christ as a sinner's Savior. Come, then, sinners; take Him, accept Him, and rest in Him. Oh, how foolish we are when we begin raising questions, objections, and difficulties! God declares that Christ is a Savior to all who trust in Him. My poor heart trusts Him; it has peace. But why do some of you imagine that He cannot save you? Why do you ask, "How can it be that this man would save me?" God has appointed Him. Take Him; rest in Him.

Moreover, God has qualified Him and given Him the anointing of a Savior. What? Do you think that God has not given Him enough power or furnished Him with enough merit with which to save such as you are? Will you limit what God has done? Will you think that His anointing is imperfect and cannot qualify Jesus to remedy your condition? Oh, do not slander the grace of heaven! Do not insult the wisdom of the Lord! Honor the Savior of God's anointing by coming now, just as you are, and putting your trust in Him.

HIS MEMORABLE ATTRIBUTE

Jesus Christ is said to be *"the same."* Now, as far as His circumstances are concerned, He has not been the same at all times, for He was once adored by angels but afterward spit on by men. He exchanged the heavenly splendors of His Father's court for the poverty of the earth, the degradation of death, and the humiliation of the grave.

Jesus Christ is not, and will not, always be the same in regard to His occupation. Once He came *"to seek and to save that which was lost"* (Luke 19:10), but we very truly sing, "The Lord will come, but not the same as once in lowliness He came." He will come again with a very different purpose. He will come to scatter His enemies and to break them as with a rod of iron (Ps. 2:9).

Therefore, we are not to interpret the expression *"the same"* in the strictest sense imaginable. Looking at the original Greek, I notice that our text might be read this way: "Jesus Christ Himself, yesterday and today and forever." The anointed Savior is always Himself. He is always Jesus Christ. The word *same* seems to me to have the most intimate relationship with the two titles of the text. Jesus Christ is always Jesus Christ, yesterday and today and forever. Jesus Christ is always Himself. At any rate, if that is not the correct translation, it is a very correct and blessed statement. It is sweetly true that Jesus Christ is always Himself.

The Same Yesterday

An unchangeable nature is ascribed to Christ, and He was always to His people what He is now, for He was *"the same yesterday."*

Some men who are extremely wise (at least in their own opinion) have drawn distinctions between the people of God who lived before the coming of Christ and those who lived afterward. I have even heard it said that those who lived before the coming of Christ do not belong to the church of God. We never know what we will hear next, and perhaps it is a mercy that these absurdities are revealed one at a time, so that we may be able to endure their stupidity without dying of amazement.

Why, every child of God in every place stands on the same footing. The Lord does not have some children whom He loves the best, some who are second-rate, and others whom He hardly cares about. Those who saw Christ's day before it came differ greatly from us as far as what they knew, and perhaps to that extent, they differ as far as what they enjoyed in meditating on Christ while they were on earth.

But they were all washed in the same blood, all redeemed with the same ransom price, and all made members of the same body. In the covenant of grace, the Israel of God is not natural Israel, but all believers from all ages.

Before the First Advent, all the types and shadows pointed one way—to Christ. To Him all believers looked with hope. Those who lived before Christ were not saved with a different salvation than the eternal salvation that will come to us. They exercised faith just as we must. Their faith struggled as ours struggles, and their faith obtained its eternal reward just as ours will. Comparing the spiritual life of the believer now with the spiritual life of David is like comparing a man's face with a reflection of that face.

Sometime, when you are reading the book of Psalms, forget for an instant that you are reading about the life of someone who lived a long time ago. You might suppose that David wrote only yesterday. Even in what he wrote about Christ, it seems as though he lived after Christ, instead of before. Furthermore, both in what he saw of himself and of his Savior, he sounds more like a New Testament believer who has found his Messiah than an Old Testament Israelite still awaiting the Christ. What I am saying is that, living before Christ, he had the same hopes and the same fears, the same joys and the same sorrows. He had the same impression of his blessed Redeemer that you and I have in these times. Jesus was the same yesterday as He is today, as far as being an anointed Savior to His people. They received from Him similar precious gifts. If the good prophets could be here today, they would all testify that in every office, He was the same in their time as He is today.

The Same Today

Jesus Christ is the same now as He was in the past, for the text says, *"The same yesterday, and to day."* He is the same today as He has been from eternity. Before all the worlds existed, He planned our salvation, and He entered into covenant with His Father to undertake it. His *"delights were with the sons of men"* (Prov. 8:31) who would one day inhabit the earth, and now today He is as faithful to that covenant as ever. He will not lose those who were then given to Him (John 18:9), nor will He fail or be discouraged, for every stipulation of that covenant will be fulfilled. The same infinite love that was in the heart of Christ before the stars began to shine is there today.

Jesus is the same today as He was when He was here on earth. There is much comfort in this thought. When He lived among men, He was most willing to save. *"Come unto me, all ye that labour and are heavy laden"* (Matt. 11:28) was His cry. He is still calling to the weary and the burdened to come to Him. When He was on earth, He would not curse the woman caught in adultery, nor would He reject the tax collectors and sinners who gathered to hear Him. He is still merciful to sinners, and He still says to them, *"Neither do I condemn thee: go, and sin no more"* (John 8:11). That delightful sentence that so graciously came from His lips—"[Your] *sins, which are many, are forgiven"* (Luke 7:47)—is still His favorite utterance to human hearts.

Oh, do not think that Christ in heaven has become distant and reserved, so that you may not approach Him. He is the same now as He was when He lived here—a Lamb, gentle and meek, a Man to whom men drew near without a moment's hesitation. Come boldly to Him, you lowliest and guiltiest ones. Come near to Him with broken hearts and weeping eyes. Though He is King and Priest, surrounded with inconceivable splendor, yet He has the same loving heart and the same generous sympathy for the sons of men.

He is still the same in His ability as well as in His willingness to save. He is still Jesus Christ, the anointed Savior. In His earthly days, He touched the leper and said, *"I will; be thou clean"* (Matt. 8:3). He called Lazarus from the tomb, and Lazarus came. Sinner, Jesus is still just as able to heal or enliven you as He was able to do for others then. *"He is able also to save them to the uttermost that come unto God by him, seeing he ever liveth to make intercession for them"* (Heb. 7:25). Now that His blood has been shed indeed, and the sacrifice has been fully offered, there is no limit to the ability of Christ to save. Oh, come and rely on Him, and find salvation in Him now.

Believer, it will encourage you also to remember that when our Lord was here on earth, He showed great perseverance in His art of saving. He could say, *"Of them which thou gavest me have I lost none"* (John 18:9). Rejoice that He is the same today. He will not cast one of you away or allow His little ones to perish. He kept all safe in the days of His earthly sojourn; He takes care to keep all safe now in the days of His heavenly glory. He is the same today as He was while on earth.

Blessed be His name; Jesus Christ is the same today as in apostolic days. Then He gave the fullness of the Spirit; then, *"when he ascended up on high, he...gave gifts unto men"* (Eph. 4:8)—apostles, preachers, teachers of the Word (v. 11). Do not think that we will never see days as good as the Day of Pentecost. He is the same Christ. He could just as readily convert three thousand after one sermon today as in Peter's time. His Holy Spirit is not exhausted, for *"God giveth not the Spirit by measure unto* [Christ]" (John 3:34).

We ought to pray that God would raise up among us prominent men to proclaim the Gospel. We do not pray enough for the ministry. The ministry is the particular gift of the Ascension. When Jesus Christ ascended on high, He received gifts for men, and He gave what? Why, apostles, teachers, preachers. When we ask for salvation, we plead the blood of Jesus; why don't we ask for ministers and plead the Ascension? If we would do this more, we would see raised up among us more Whitefields and Wesleys, more Luthers and Calvins, more men of the apostolic kind. Then the church would be revived. Jesus Christ, being the same, is able to enrich His people with all spiritual gifts this year just as in the year when He ascended to His throne. He is *"the same yesterday, and to day."*

He is the same today as He was to our forefathers in the faith. They have gone to their rest, but they testified before they went of what Christ had been to them, how He had helped them in their time of peril, how He had delivered them in their hour of sorrow. He will do for us just what He did for them. Some who lived before us were burned at the stake for their faith, but Christ was very precious to them as they went to heaven in chariots of fire. We read the stories of Christian martyrs with wonder. How sustaining the presence of Christ was to those who lay in prison, to those who were thrown to the lions, to those who wandered around in sheepskins and goatskins! England, Scotland—all the countries where Christ has been preached—have been dyed with the blood and ennobled with the testimonies of the faithful. Whatever Jesus was to these worthy believers who have now departed, He is to His people still. We only have to ask God, and we will receive the very same benefits.

"Jesus Christ the same...to day," says the text. Therefore, He is the same today as He has been to us in the past. We have greatly enjoyed God's presence. We remember the love of our first days of salvation, and if we do not have the same joys today, it is no fault of His. The same water is still in the well; if we have not drawn it, it is our own fault. We have walked away from the fire, and therefore we are cold. We have walked contrary to Him, and therefore He walks contrary to us (Lev. 26:23–24). Let us return to Him, and He will be as glad to receive us now as in our first moment of repentance. Let us return to Him. His heart is just as full of love, and He is just as ready to tearfully embrace us as when we first came and sought pardon from His hands.

There are many precious truths in the text, but I cannot linger any longer on this part of the subject. It is enough for us to remember that Jesus Christ is the same today as He always has been.

The Same Forever

Lastly, Christ will be tomorrow what He was yesterday and is today. Our Lord Jesus Christ will be changed in no respect throughout the duration of our lives. It may be a long time before we descend to our graves. Let these hairs of mine all turn gray, and these legs of mine begin to wobble, and these eyes of mine grow dim, for Jesus Christ will have the dew of His youth upon Him (Ps. 110:3), and the fullness of His love will still flow to me. And after death, or, if we do not die, at the coming of Christ and in His glorious reign, Jesus will be the same to His people as He is now.

It seems that an idea is being circulated that after His coming, Christ will deal differently with His people than now. I have been informed by a contemporary school of inventors of religion, who invent newfangled ideas, that some of us will be shut out of the kingdom when Christ comes. Saved by precious blood and brought near to God, adopted into the family, our names written on the breastplate of Christ, we will be shut out from the kingdom! Nonsense. I see nothing about this in the Word of God, though there might be a great deal of it in the imaginations of people.

The people of God, equally bought with blood and equally dear to Jesus' heart, will be treated on the same scale and footing. They will never be put under the law; they will never come to Christ in a future state and find Him ruling them as a legal Judge, beating them with many lashes, or shutting them out of His estate of millennial majesty. He will not reward some by giving them rule and authority and at the same time exclude others of His redeemed family. His entire family will find that He always treats them as unchanging love and immutable grace dictate.

The rewards of the millennial state will always be those of grace; they will not be such that they will exclude even the very least of God's family. In fact, all believers will receive rewards from the dear Savior's hand. I know He will not love me today, giving me glimpses of His face and allowing me to delight in His name, and yet, after He comes, tell me I cannot enter His kingdom but must stand out in the cold. I do not have a shade of faith in this "purgatory" of banishment, which certain despisers of the ministry have chosen to set up. I marvel that in a Protestant denomination there should rise up a dogma as villainous as the dogma of purgatory. These teachers say that everyone else is wrong but that they have been taught deep things and can discover what the best theologians have never seen.

I know this: Jesus will love His people in times to come as strongly as He does now. The destruction or denial of this doctrine would cast sorrow into the whole family of God. Throughout eternity, in heaven, there will still be the same Jesus Christ, with the same love for His people. They will have the same intimate communion with Him—no, they will see Him face-to-face. They will rejoice forever in Him as their unchangeably anointed Savior.

OUR LORD'S CLAIMS UPON US

Since our Lord is *"the same yesterday, and to day, and for ever,"* then, according to the verse preceding our text, He is to be followed to the end. Observe the seventh verse: *"Remember them which have the rule over you, who have spoken unto you the word of God: whose faith follow, considering the end of their conversation"* (Heb. 13:7). The meaning of the verse is this: these holy men ended their lives with Christ; their exit out of this life meant going to Jesus and reigning with Him. Beloved, if the Lord is still the same, follow Him until you reach Him. Your exit out of this life will bring you where He is, and you will find Him to be then what He always was. You will *"see him as he is"* (1 John 3:2). If He were a delusive hope, forever changing, it would be dangerous to follow Him. But since He is always equally worthy of your admiration and imitation, follow Him forever.

Henry VI of France gave an eloquent speech on the eve of a certain battle. He said to his soldiers, "Gentlemen, you are Frenchmen. I am your king. There is the enemy!" Similarly, Jesus Christ says, "You are my people. I am your leader. There is the foe!" How dare we do anything unworthy of such a Lord as He is, or of such a citizenship as that which He has given us? If we are indeed His, and He is indeed immutable, let us by His Holy Spirit's power persevere to the end, so that we may obtain the crown.

The next claim of Christ upon us is that we should be steadfast in the faith. Notice the verse after our text: *"Be not carried about with divers [various] and strange doctrines"* (Heb. 13:9). There is nothing new in theology except that which is false. All that is true is old, though I am not saying that all that is old is true. Some speak of new developments as though we had not discovered the whole Christian religion yet. But the religion of Paul is the religion of every person who is taught by the Holy Spirit. We must not, therefore, indulge for a moment the idea that something has been discovered that might correct the teaching of Christ, that some new philosophy or scientific discovery has arisen to correct the declared testimony of our Redeemer. Let us hold tightly to what we have received; let us never depart from *"the faith which was once delivered unto the saints"* (Jude 3) by Christ Himself.

Moreover, since Jesus Christ is immutable, He has an obvious claim to our most solemn worship. Immutability can be the attribute of no one but God. Whoever is *"the same yesterday, and to day, and for ever"* must be divine. Forever, then, believer, bring your adoration to Jesus. At the feet of Him who was crucified, cast your crown. Give royal and divine honors to the One who stooped to the ignominy of crucifixion. Let no one prevent you from glorying in Christ, for you boast in the Son of God made man for you. Worship Him as God over all, blessed forever.

Next, He has a claim to our trust. If He is always the same, here is a rock that cannot be moved. Build on it! Here is a haven. Cast your anchor of hope into it, and hold on in times of storm. If Christ were changeable, He would not be worthy of your confidence. But, since He is forever unchanged, rest on Him without fear.

Lastly, if He is always the same, rejoice in Him, and rejoice always. If you have ever had cause to rejoice in Christ, you always have cause, for He never changes. If yesterday you could sing of Him, today you may sing of Him. If He were subject to change, your joy might change. But if the stream of your gladness springs solely out of this great deep of the immutability of Jesus, then it never needs to stop flowing. Beloved, let us *"rejoice in the Lord alway: and again I say, Rejoice"* (Phil. 4:4). Until the day breaks and the shadows flee away, until the blessed hour arrives when we will see Him face-to-face and be made like Him, let this be our joy, that He is *"the same yesterday, and to day, and for ever."*

Chapter 6

Suffering and Reigning with Jesus

If we suffer, we shall also reign with him: if we deny him, he also will deny us.
—2 Timothy 2:12

O ur text is the second part of one of Paul's faithful sayings. If I remember correctly, Paul had four of these. The first occurs in 1 Timothy 1:15, that famous, that foremost of all faithful sayings: *"This is a faithful saying, and worthy of all acceptation, that Christ Jesus came into the world to save sinners; of whom I am chief."* Paul himself had most marvelously proved the value of this golden saying. What should I say about this verse except that, like the light of a lighthouse, it has darted its ray of comfort through miles of darkness and has guided millions of tempest-tossed spirits to the port of peace?

The next faithful saying is in the same epistle:

> *Godliness is profitable unto all things, having promise of the life that now is, and of that which is to come. This is a faithful saying and worthy of all acceptation.* *(1 Tim. 4:8–9)*

This, too, the apostle knew to be true, since he had learned *"in whatsoever state* [he was], *therewith to be content"* (Phil. 4:11).

Our text is a portion of the third faithful saying. The last of the four you will find in Titus:

> *This is a faithful saying, and these things I will that thou affirm constantly, that they which have believed in God might be careful to maintain good works. These things are good and profitable unto men.* *(Titus 3:8)*

There is a connection between these faithful sayings. The first one, which speaks of Jesus Christ coming into the world to save sinners, lays the foundation of our eternal salvation, which is the free grace of God. This grace was shown to us in the mission of the great Redeemer. The next faithful saying affirms the double blessedness that we obtain through this salvation—the blessings of both the lower and upper springs—of both time and eternity. The third faithful saying shows one of the duties to which the chosen people are called: we are ordained to suffer for Christ with the promise that *"if we suffer, we shall also reign with him."* The last faithful saying describes the active form of Christian service, instructing us to diligently maintain good works.

Thus you have, first, the root of salvation in free grace; next, the privileges of that salvation in the present life and in the life to come; and, lastly, the two great branches of suffering with Christ and service to Christ, loaded with the fruits of the Spirit of all grace.

Treasure up, dear friend, these faithful sayings. *"Lay up these my words in your heart and in your soul, and bind them for a sign upon your hand, that they may be as frontlets between your eyes"* (Deut. 11:18). Let these choice sayings be printed in letters of gold and posted on the doorposts of our houses and on our gates (v. 20). Let them be the guides of our lives, as well as our comfort and our instruction. The Apostle to the Gentiles proved them to be faithful. They are faithful still. Not one word will fall to the ground. They are worthy of full acceptance. Let us accept them now and prove their faithfulness.

This chapter will focus on a part of the faithful saying that deals with suffering. Let us look at the verse preceding our text: *"It is a faithful saying: for if we be dead with him, we shall also live with him"* (2 Tim. 2:11). All the elect were virtually dead with Christ when He died on the cross; they were on the cross, crucified with Him (Gal. 2:20). In Him, who is their Representative, they rose from the tomb, and they live in *"newness of life"* (Rom. 6:4). Because He lives, they will live also (John 14:19).

In due time, the chosen are drawn to God by the Spirit of God. When they are saved, they are made dead with Christ to sin, to self-righteousness, to the world, to the flesh, and to the powers of darkness. Then it is that they live with Jesus; His life becomes their life. As He was, so are they also in this world (1 John 4:17). The Spirit of God breathes the quickening grace into those who were once dead in sin, and thus they live in union with Christ Jesus. A believer may be sawed in half or burned at the stake. Yet, since he sleeps in Jesus, he is preserved from the destruction of death by Him; he is made a partaker of Christ's immortality. May the Lord root us and ground us in the mysterious but most comforting doctrine of union with Christ Jesus.

Let us now focus on our text: *"If we suffer, we shall also reign with him: if we deny him, he also will deny us."* The words naturally divide themselves into two parts: first, suffering with Jesus and its reward; second, denying Jesus and its penalty.

SUFFERING WITH JESUS AND ITS REWARD

To suffer is the common lot of all people. It is not possible for us to escape from pain. We come into this world through the gate of suffering, and we leave it through the same gate. We suffer if we live, regardless of what kind of lives we lead. The wicked individual may cast off all respect for virtue; he may live riotously in excessive vice. Yet, he must not expect to avoid the well-directed shafts of sorrow. No, rather let him expect a tenfold share of bodily pain and remorse of soul. *"Many sorrows shall be to the wicked"* (Ps. 32:10). Even if a person could so completely degrade himself as to lose his intellectual powers and become like an animal, even then he could not escape from suffering, for we know that the animal is the victim of pain as much as more lordly man. In fact, the animals have the additional misery that they have no mind endowed with reason or encouraged by hope to fortify them in their pain.

Oh, man, don't you see that however you may degrade yourself, you are still under the yoke of suffering? The loftiest men bow beneath it, and the lowest men cannot avoid it. Every acre of humanity must be furrowed with this plow. There may be a sea without a wave, but never a man without a sorrow. He who was God as well as man, had His full measure of pain; in fact, His share was pressed down and running over. Let us be assured that if the Sinless One was not spared the rod, the sinful will not go free. *"Man that is born of a woman is of few days, and full of trouble"* (Job 14:1). *"Man is born unto trouble, as the sparks fly upward"* (Job 5:7).

Suffering That Does Not Ensure a Reward

If, then, a man has sorrow, it does not necessarily mean that he will be rewarded for it, since it is the common lot brought upon all by sin. You may ache under the lashes of sorrow in this life, but your sadness will not deliver you from the wrath to come. Remember, you may live in poverty and lead a wearisome life of unrewarded toil. You may be placed on a sickbed and be made to experience agony in every part of your body. Your mind, too, may be depressed with fears or plunged into the depths of despair. Yet, by all this, you may gain nothing of any value to your immortal spirit. *"Except a man be born again, he cannot see the kingdom of God"* (John 3:3), and no amount of affliction on earth can alter that unchanging rule to admit an unsaved person into heaven.

To suffer is not unique to the Christian. Nor does suffering necessarily bring with it any reward. The text clearly implies that we must suffer *with Christ* in order to reign with Him. The structure of our text plainly requires such a reading. The words *"with him"* may be as accurately placed at the end of the one clause as the other: *"If we suffer* [with Him], *we shall also reign with him."* The suffering that brings the reigning with Jesus, must be a suffering with Jesus.

There is a misconception among many poor people who are ignorant of true Christianity, that all poor and afflicted people will be rewarded for their suffering in the next state. I have heard workingmen refer to the parable of the rich man and Lazarus (Luke 16:19–31) with a cruel sort of satisfaction at the pains of the rich man. They have imagined that, in the same manner, all rich people will be cast into the flames of hell without a drop of water to cool their tongues, while all poor people like Lazarus will be triumphantly carried into Abraham's bosom.

A more fearful mistake could not be made. It was not the suffering of Lazarus that entitled him to a place in Abraham's bosom. He might have been licked by all the dogs on earth and then dragged off by the dogs of hell. Many a man goes to hell a pauper. A drunkard's hut is very wretched; is he to be rewarded for bringing himself to rags? Very much of the poverty we see around us is the result of vice, extravagance, or folly. Are these things so meritorious as to be passports to glory? Let no man deceive himself so horribly.

On the other hand, the rich man was not cast into hell because he was rich and lived luxuriously. Had he been rich in faith, holy in life, and renewed in heart, his purple and fine linen would have done him no harm. Lazarus was carried above by the angels because his heart was in heaven, and the rich man lifted up his eyes in hell because he had never lifted them up toward God and heavenly things.

It is a work of grace in the heart and character that will decide the future, not poverty or wealth. Suffering here does not imply happiness hereafter. Let sensible people combat this false idea whenever they encounter it. It is only a certain type of suffering to which a reward is promised—the suffering that comes to us from fellowship with the Lord Jesus and conformity to His image.

The Necessity of Being in Christ

Let me add a few words here to help you in making the distinction between these two types of suffering. We must not imagine that we are suffering for Christ, and with Christ, if we are not in Christ. If a person is not a branch of the Living Vine, you may prune and cut until the branch bleeds and the sap flows, but he will never bring forth heavenly fruit. Prune the bramble as long as you like—use the knife until the edge is worn away—but the brier will be as sharp and fruitless as ever. No process of pruning will transform the brier into one of the vines of Eshcol (Num. 13:23).

In the same way, if a person remains in a fallen state, he is a member of the earthly Adam. He will not therefore escape suffering, but ensure it. He must not, however, dream that because he suffers, he is suffering with Christ. He is plagued with the old Adam. He is receiving, with all the other heirs of wrath, the sure heritage of sin. Let him consider these sufferings of his to be only the first drops of the awful shower that will fall upon him forever, the first tingling cuts of that terrible whip that will lacerate his soul forever.

However, if a person is in Christ, he may then claim fellowship with the Second Man, who is the Lord from heaven. He may expect to bear the image of the heavenly in the glory to be revealed. Oh, my reader, are you in Christ by a living faith? Are you trusting in Jesus alone? If not, regardless of what you may have to mourn over on earth, you have no hope of reigning with Jesus in heaven.

Suffering Caused by Our Own Mistakes

Even when a man is in Christ, it does not mean that all his sufferings are sufferings with Christ, for it is essential that he be called by God to suffer. If a good man were, out of mistaken views of dying to self and self-denial, to mutilate his body or to flog his flesh, as many a sincere enthusiast has done, I might admire the man's fortitude, but I would not believe for an instant that he was suffering with Christ. Who called men to such severities? Certainly not the God of love. If, therefore, they torture themselves at the command of their own inclinations, inclination must reward them, for God will not.

If I am rash and imprudent and run into situations for which neither providence nor grace has prepared me, I ought to question whether I am not sinning rather than communing with Christ. Peter drew his sword and cut off the ear of Malchus. (See John 18:3–5, 10–11.) If somebody had cut off Peter's ear in return, what would you say? You would say that Peter used the sword, and therefore he felt the sword. He was never commanded to cut off the ear of Malchus, and it was his Master's gentleness that saved him from the soldiers' rage. If we let passion take the place of judgment, if we let self-will reign instead of scriptural authority, we will fight the Lord's battles with the Devil's weapons, and we must not be surprised if we cut off our own fingers.

On several occasions, excited Protestants have rushed into Catholic cathedrals, knocked down the priest, dashed the wafer to the ground, trod on it, and in other ways exhibited their hatred of idolatry. Now, when the law has intervened to punish such outrages, the offenders are hardly to be considered as suffering with Christ.

This I give as one example of a kind of action to which overheated brains sometimes lead people, under the supposition that they will join the noble army of martyrs. The martyrs were all chosen to their honorable estate. I may say of martyrdom, as of priesthood, *"No man taketh this honour unto himself, but he that is called of God, as was Aaron"* (Heb. 5:4). Let us be careful that we make proper distinctions, that we do not pull a house down on our heads and then ask the Lord to console us under the trial.

Again, in troubles that come upon us as the result of sin, we must not think that we are suffering with Christ. When Miriam spoke evil of Moses and leprosy polluted her, she was not suffering for God. When Uzziah went into the temple to burn incense and became a leper all his days, he could not say that he was afflicted for righteousness' sake. If you speculate and lose your property, do not say that you are losing all for Christ's sake. When you invest in shaky companies and are duped, do not whine about suffering for Christ—call it the fruit of your own folly. If you put your hand into the fire, do not complain if you get burned; why, it is the nature of fire to burn you or anybody else. Do not be so silly as to boast as though you were a martyr. If you do wrong and suffer for it, what thanks do you have (1 Pet. 2:20)? Hide your face and weep for your sin, but do not come forth in public to claim a reward.

Many a hypocrite, when he has had his just deserts and has been called by his proper name, has cried out, "I am persecuted." However, it is not, as some believe, an infallible sign of excellence to have a bad reputation. Who feels any esteem for a cold-blooded murderer? Doesn't every man condemn the offender? Is he, therefore, a Christian because he is spoken against and rejected? Assuredly not; he is a heartless villain and nothing more.

Beloved, honesty should stop us from making false claims. We must not talk as if we are suffering nobly for Jesus when we are only troubled as the result of sin. Oh, to be kept from transgression! Then it does not matter how rough the road of obedience may be; our journey will be pleasant because Jesus walks with us.

The Right Motives and Attitudes

Observe, moreover, that the suffering that God accepts and rewards, for Christ's sake, must have God's glory as its goal. If I suffer so that I may earn a name or win applause from others, if I undergo a trial merely so that I may be respected for it, I will get my reward, but it will be the reward of the Pharisee and not the crown of the sincere servant of the Lord Jesus.

I must be careful, too, that love for Christ and love for His elect are always the mainspring of all my patience in suffering. Remember the apostle's words: *"Though I give my body to be burned, and have not charity, it profiteth me nothing"* (1 Cor. 13:3). If I suffer in bravado, filled with proud defiance of my fellowmen; if I love the dignity of singularity, and out of dogged obstinacy hold to an opinion—not because it is right and I love God too much to deny His truth, but because I choose to think as I like—then I do not suffer with Jesus. If there is no love for God in my soul, if I do not endure all things for the elect's sake, I may bear many a slap and beating, but I miss the fellowship of the Spirit and have no reward.

Also, I must not forget that I must manifest the attitude of Christ or else I do not suffer with Him. I once heard about a certain minister who, having had a disagreement with several members in his church, preached from this text: *"And Aaron held his peace"*

(Lev. 10:3). He preached the sermon with the intention of portraying himself as an astonishing example of meekness, but since his previous words and actions had been quite violent, a witty hearer observed that the only likeness he could see between Aaron and the preacher was this: "*'Aaron held his peace,'* and the preacher did not." It is easy enough to discover some parallel between our situations and those of departed believers, but not so easy to carry out the parallel by holy patience and Christlike forgiveness.

If I have brought upon myself shame and rebuke; if I am quick to defend myself and to punish the slanderer; if I am irritated, unforgiving, and proud, I have lost a noble opportunity of fellowship with Jesus. If I do not have Christ's attitudes in me, I do not suffer acceptably. If, like a sheep before her shearers, I can be silent (Isa. 53:7); if I can bear insult and love the man who inflicts it; if I can pray with Christ, *"Father, forgive them; for they know not what they do"* (Luke 23:34); if I submit my whole situation to Him who judges righteously; if I consider it my joy to suffer reproach for the cause of Christ, then, and only then, have I truly suffered with Christ.

These remarks may seem very cutting. They may take away much false but highly prized comfort from you. It is not my intention to take away any true comfort from the humblest believer who really suffers with my Lord. But may God grant that we may have enough honesty not to pluck flowers out of other men's gardens or wear other men's honors. Only truth will be desired by true men.

The Sufferers Who Will Receive a Reward

I will now very briefly discuss the ways in which we may suffer for Jesus in our day. It is not our lot now to rot in prisons, to wander around in sheepskins and goatskins, to be stoned, or to be sawed in half, though we ought to be ready to bear all this if God wills it. The days of Nebuchadnezzar's furnace are past, but the fire is still on earth.

Some, for instance, suffer in their finances. I admit that many Christians gain financially rather than lose financially when they become believers in Christ. But I encounter many cases—cases that I know to be genuine—in which Christians have had to suffer severely for conscience' sake. I know people who were once in very comfortable circumstances, but they lived in a neighborhood where most of the business was done on Sundays. When they became Christians and closed their shops on Sundays, their customers left them. I know that some of them are working very hard for their bread, though once they earned abundance without any great toil. They do it cheerfully for Christ's sake, but the struggle is a hard one.

I know other people who were once employed in lucrative jobs, but their jobs involved sin. When they became Christians, they were obliged to resign. Now they do not have anything like the apparent prosperity they used to have. Their incomes have been significantly reduced.

I could point to several cases of people who have truly suffered greatly in financial matters for the Cross of Christ. If this is your situation, you may possess your soul by patience (Luke 21:19) and expect as a reward of grace that you will reign with Jesus, your Beloved.

Those featherbed soldiers who are broken-hearted if fools laugh at them, should blush when they think of those who endure real hardship as good soldiers of Jesus Christ. Who can waste his pity over the small griefs of faint hearts, when cold, hunger, and poverty are cheerfully endured by the true and the brave? Cases of persecution are by no means rare. We who live in a more enlightened society little know the terrorism exercised in some places over poor men and women who endeavor conscientiously to carry out their convictions and walk with Christ. To all saints who are oppressed, this sweet sentence is directed: *"If we suffer, we shall also reign with him."*

More often, however, the Christian's suffering takes the form of personal contempt. It is not pleasant to be pointed at in the streets and have disgraceful names shouted after you by vulgar tongues. Nor is it a small trial to be greeted in the workplace by reproachful names, or to be looked upon as an idiot or a madman. Yet this is the lot of many people of God every day of the week. Many of those who are of the humbler classes have to endure constant and open reproach, and those who are richer have to put up with the cold shoulder, neglect, and sneers as soon as they become true disciples of Jesus Christ. There is more sting in this than some imagine. I have known strong men who could have borne the whip but were brought down by jeers and sarcasm. Indeed, a lion may be more troubled by the irritations of a wasp than by the attack of the noblest beast of prey.

Believers also have to suffer slander and falsehood. Undoubtedly, it is not profitable for me to boast, but I know a man who scarcely ever speaks a word that is not misrepresented, or performs an action that is not misconstrued. At certain seasons, the press, like a pack of hounds, will get on his trail, harassing him with the vilest and most undeserved abuse. Publicly and privately, he is accustomed to being sneered at. The world whispers, "Oh, he pretends to be zealous for God, but he makes a fine show of it!" Mind you, when the people of the world do learn what he makes of it, maybe they will have to eat their words.

However, I will not focus on myself, for such is the portion of every servant of God who publicly testifies to the truth. Every motive but the right one will be imputed to him. His good will be spoken of as evil; his zeal will be called imprudence; his courage, impertinence; his modesty, cowardice; his earnestness, rashness. It is impossible for the true believer in Christ who is called to any prominent service to do anything right in the eyes of the world. He had better learn right now to say with Luther, "The world hates me, and there is no love lost between us, for as much as it hates me, so heartily do I hate it." He did not mean that he hated the people in the world, for never was there a more loving heart than Luther's. But he meant that he hated the fame, the opinion, the honor of the world. If, in your measure, you bear undeserved rebuke for Christ's sake, comfort yourself with these words: *"If we suffer, we shall also reign with him: if we deny him, he also will deny us."*

If, in your service for Christ, you are enabled to sacrifice yourself in such a way that you bring upon yourself inconvenience and pain, labor and loss, then I think you are suffering with Christ. The missionary penetrating into unknown regions among savages, the teacher going wearily to class, the village preacher walking many toilsome miles, the minister starving on a miserable pittance, the evangelist content to deteriorate in health—all these, and those like them, suffer with Christ.

We are all too occupied with taking care of ourselves. We shun the difficulties of excessive labor. Frequently, because we are too concerned about caring for our health, we do not do half as much as we ought. A minister of God must spurn the suggestion to take it easy; it is his calling to labor. If he destroys his health, I, for one, only thank God that He permits us the high privilege of making ourselves living sacrifices. If earnest ministers bring themselves to the grave, not by imprudence, for that I would not advocate, but by the honest labor that their ministries and their consciences require of them, they will be better in their graves than out of them. What? Are we never to suffer? Are we to be summer soldiers? Are God's people to be pampered—perfumed with fragrances and indulged with quiet softnesses? Certainly not, unless they want to lose the reward of true saints!

In addition, let us not forget that war with our own lusts, denials of proud self, resistance of sin, and agony against Satan, are all forms of suffering with

Christ. We may, in the holy war within us, earn as bright a crown as in the wider battlefield beyond us. Oh, for grace to be always dressed in full armor, fighting with principalities and powers, as well as spiritual wickedness of every sort.

I will mention one more type of suffering, that is, friends forsaking us or becoming our foes. Father and mother sometimes forsake their children. The husband sometimes persecutes the wife. I have even known the children to turn against the parents. *"A man's foes* [are] *they of his own household"* (Matt. 10:36). This is one of the Devil's best instruments for making believers suffer, and those who have to drain this cup for the Lord's sake will reign with Him.

Beloved, if you are called to suffer for Christ in this way, will you quarrel with me if I say, in adding up all your sufferings, what very little they are compared with reigning with Jesus? *"For our light affliction, which is but for a moment, worketh for us a far more exceeding and eternal weight of glory"* (2 Cor. 4:17). When I contrast our sufferings of today with the sufferings of Christians in pagan Rome, why, ours are scarcely a thimbleful! Yet what is our reward? We will reign with Christ. There is no comparison between the service and the reward. Therefore, it is all of grace. We do only a little and suffer only a little, and it is grace that gives us that little bit. Yet the Lord grants us *"a far more exceeding and eternal weight of glory."*

We will not merely sit with Christ; we will reign with Christ. All the royal splendor of His kingship, all the treasure of His wide dominions, all the majesty of His everlasting power—all this is to belong to you. It will be given to you by His rich, free grace as the sweet reward of having suffered for a little while with Him.

Who would draw back, then? Who would flinch? Young man, have you thought about running from the cross? Young woman, has Satan whispered to you to shun the thorny pathway? Will you give up the crown? Will you miss the throne? Oh, beloved, it is so blessed to be in the furnace with Christ, it is such an honor to be publicly humiliated with Him, that if there were no reward, we could consider ourselves happy. But when the reward is so rich, so superabundant, so eternal, so infinitely more than we had any right to expect, will we not take up the cross with songs and go on our way rejoicing in the Lord our God?

DENYING CHRIST AND ITS PENALTY

"If we deny him, he also will deny us." That is a dreadful *"if,"* yet an *"if"* that is applicable to every individual. The apostles, in response to Christ's statement that one of them would betray Him, asked, *"Lord, is it I?"* (Matt. 26:22). In the same way, surely we may ask, "Lord, will I ever deny You?" You who say most loudly, *"Though all men shall be offended because of thee, yet will I never be offended"* (v. 33)— you are the most likely to deny Christ.

Ways That People Deny Christ

In what ways can we deny Christ? Scoffers deny Him openly. *"They set their mouth against the* heavens, and their tongue walketh through the earth" (Ps. 73:9). Others deny Him willfully and wickedly in a doctrinal way. Take, for example, those who deny His deity. Also, those who deny His atonement and those who speak against the inspiration of His Word come under the condemnation of those who deny Christ.

In addition, there is a way of denying Christ without even saying a word, and this is more common. When blasphemy and rebuke are encountered, many hide their heads. They are in company where they ought to speak up for Christ, but they put their hands over their mouths. They do not come forward to profess their faith in Jesus. They have a kind of faith, but it is one that yields no obedience. Jesus instructs each believer to be baptized, but they neglect His ordinance. Neglecting that, they also despise *the weightier matters of the law*" (Matt. 23:23).

They go to the house of God because it is fashionable to go there, but if it were a matter of persecution, they would forsake *the assembling of* [themselves] *together*" (Heb. 10:25). In the day of battle, they are never on the Lord's side. If there is a parade and the banners are flying and the trumpets are sounding, if there are decorations and medals to be given away, they are there. But if shots are flying, if trenches have to be dug, if fortresses have to be stormed, where are they? They have gone back to their dens, and there they will hide themselves until fair weather returns.

Pay attention, for I am giving a description, I am afraid, of many people. Pay attention, I say, you silent one, lest you stand speechless at the judgment seat of Christ.

Some who have been practically denying Christ for a long time by their silence go even further. They apostatize altogether from the faith they once had. No one who has a genuine faith in Christ will lose it, for the faith that God gives will live forever. But hypocrites and formalists have a reputation for being alive while they are yet dead (Rev. 3:1), and after a while they return like the dog to its vomit and like the sow that was washed to her wallowing in the mire (2 Pet. 2:22).

Some do not go this far, yet they practically deny Christ by their lives, though they make a profession of faith in Him. Some are baptized and receive communion, but what is their character? Follow them home. I strongly wish that they had never made a profession, because in their own houses they deny what in the house of God they have avowed. If I see a man drunk; if I know that a man indulges in immorality; if I know a man to be harsh, overbearing, and tyrannical to his employees; if I know another who cheats his customers; and if I know that such men profess allegiance to Jesus, which am I to believe, their words or their deeds? I will believe what speaks the loudest. Since actions always speak louder than words, I will believe their actions. I believe that they are deceivers whom Jesus will deny in the end.

Many people belong in one of these categories of those who deny Jesus. Perhaps you are one of them. If so, do not be angry with me, but stand still and hear the Word of the Lord. Understand that you will not perish even if you have denied Christ, if you now run to Him for refuge. Peter denied, yet Peter is in heaven. A transient forsaking of Jesus under temptation will not result in everlasting ruin, if faith steps in and the grace of God intervenes. However, if you continue in a denial of the Savior and persevere in it, this terrible text will come upon you: *"He also will deny* [you]."

Ways That Jesus Will Deny People

In musing over the very dreadful clause that closes our text, *"He also will deny us,"* I was led to think of various ways in which Jesus will deny us. He does this sometimes on earth. Perhaps you have read about the death of Francis Spira. If you have ever read about it, you can never forget it to your dying day. Francis Spira knew the truth—he was a religious reformer of no low standing—but when threatened with death, out of fear he recanted. In a short time, he fell into despair and suffered hell on earth. His shrieks and exclamations were so horrible that their record is almost too terrible for print. His doom was a warning to the age in which he lived.

Another instance is told of one who was very earnest for Puritanism. But when times of persecution arose, he forsook his profession of faith. The scenes at his deathbed were shocking and terrible. He declared that though he sought God, heaven was shut against him; gates of brass seemed to be in his way. He was given up to overwhelming despair. At intervals he cursed, at other intervals he prayed, and so he perished without hope.

If we deny Christ, we may be delivered to such a fate. If we have stood highest in God's church yet have not been brought to Christ, or if we become apostates, our high soar will end in a deep fall. High pretensions bring down sure destruction when they come to nothing. Christ will deny such people even on earth.

There are remarkable instances of people who sought to save their lives and lost them. Richard Denton was a very zealous follower of the English reformer John Wycliffe and had been the means of the conversion of a prominent believer. But when he came to the stake, he was so afraid of the fire that he renounced everything he held and joined the Church of Rome. A short time afterward, his own house caught on fire. Going into it to save some of his money, he perished miserably, being utterly consumed by the fire that he had denied Christ in order to escape.

If I must be lost, let it be in any other way than as an apostate. If there is any distinction among the damned, it is given to those who are trees *"twice dead, plucked up by the roots"* (Jude 12), who are *"wandering stars, to whom is reserved the blackness of darkness for ever"* (v. 13). Reserved! As if nobody else were qualified to occupy that place but themselves. They are to inhabit the darkest, hottest place, because they forsook the Lord. Let us, my dear friend, prefer to lose everything than to lose Christ. Let us sooner suffer anything than lose our ease of conscience and our peace of mind.

Marcus Arethusus was commanded by Julian the Apostate to give a donation toward the rebuilding of a heathen temple that his people had torn down after being converted to Christianity. Arethusus refused to obey. Though he was an elderly man, he was stripped naked and then pierced all over with lancets and knives. The old man stood firm. He was told that if he would give one halfpenny toward the building of the temple, he could be free. If he would cast one grain of incense into the censer devoted to the false gods, he could escape. But he would not approve of idolatry in any degree. As a result, he was smeared with honey, and while his innumerable wounds were still bleeding, the bees and wasps attacked him and stung him to death. He could die, but he could not deny his Lord. Arethusus entered into the joy of his Lord, for he nobly suffered with Him.

A long time ago, when the Gospel was preached in Persia, a courtier of the king named Hamedatha embraced the faith. He was then stripped of his position, driven from the palace, and compelled to feed camels. This he did with great contentment. The king, passing by one day, saw his former favorite at his humble work, cleaning out the camels' stables. Taking pity on him, he took him into his palace, clothed him with luxurious apparel, restored him to all his former honors, and made him sit at the royal table. In the midst of the delicious feast, he asked Hamedatha to renounce his faith. The courtier, rising from the table, tore off his garments with haste, left all the delicacies behind him, and said, "Did you think that for such silly things as these I would deny my Lord and Master?" Away he went to the stable to his lowly work.

How honorable was his reaction! But how I detest the lowness of the apostate. Because of his detestable cowardice, he forsakes the bleeding Savior of Calvary to return to the miserable principles of the world that he once despised. In his fear, he bows his neck once again to the yoke of bondage. Oh, follower of the Crucified One, will you do this? You will not. You cannot. I know you cannot if the spirit of the martyrs dwells in you, and it must dwell in you if you are a child of God.

What will be the doom of those who deny Christ when they reach another world? Perhaps they will come with a sort of hope in their minds and appear before the Judge and say, "Lord, Lord, open to me."

"Who are you?" He will ask.

"Lord, I once took the Lord's Supper. Lord, I was a member of the church, but there came very hard times. Mother told me to give up religion. Father was angry. Business went poorly. I was so ridiculed that I could not stand it. Lord, I had evil acquaintances, and they tempted me. I could not resist. I was Your servant—I did love You—I always had love for You in my heart. But I could not help it. I denied You and went back to the world."

What will Jesus say? "I do not know you."

"But Lord, I want You to be my advocate."

"I do not know you!"

"But Lord, I cannot get into heaven unless You open the gate. Open it for me."

"I do not know you. I do not know you."

"But Lord, my name was in the church's membership book."

"I do not know you. I deny you."

"But won't You hear my cries?"

"You did not hear Mine. You denied Me, and I deny you."

"Lord, I will take the lowest place in heaven, if I may only enter and escape from the wrath to come."

"No, you would not take the lowest place on earth, and you will not enjoy the lowest place here. You had your choice, and you chose evil. Stick with your choice. You were filthy; be filthy still. You were unholy; be unholy still."

Oh, friend, if you do not want to see the angry face of Jesus; oh, friend, if you do not want to behold the lightning flash from His eye and hear the thunder boom from His mouth when He judges the fearful, the unbelieving, and the hypocrite; if you do not want to have your part in the lake that burns with fire and brimstone (Rev. 21:8), mightily cry to God today. Say, "Lord, hold me fast. Keep me; keep me. Help me to suffer with You, so that I may reign with You. But do not, please do not, let me deny You, lest You also deny me."

Chapter 7

Our Own Dear Shepherd

I am the good shepherd; and I know mine own,
and mine own know me, even as the Father
knoweth me, and I know the Father; and
I lay down my life for the sheep.
—John 10:14–15 RV

The Bible version used for the above verses is the Revised Version. As the passage stands in the King James Version, it reads like a number of short sentences with hardly any apparent connection:

I am the good shepherd, and know my sheep,
and am known of mine. As the Father knoweth
me, even so know I the Father: and I lay down
my life for the sheep.

Even in that form it is precious, for our Lord's pearls are priceless even when they are not threaded together. But when I point out that the translators left out one of the *and*s in the verse, you will see that they were not too accurate in this case. Admittedly, it was John's style to use many *and*s, but there is usually a true and natural connection between his sentences. With him, the *and* is usually a golden link, not a mere sound. We need a translation that treats it this way.

It is also helpful to know that the word *sheep*, which appears in verse fourteen in the King James Version, is not in the original; it was added by the translators. However, there is no need for this alteration if the passage is more closely rendered.

Again, the Revised Version gives the text in its natural form:

> *I am the good shepherd; and I know mine own, and mine own know me, even as the Father knoweth me, and I know the Father; and I lay down my life for the sheep.*

I admit that I do not care much for the Revised Version of the New Testament as a general rule, considering it to be by no means an improvement on the King James Version. It is a useful thing to have for private reference, but I trust it will never be regarded as the standard English translation of the New Testament. The Revised Version of the Old Testament is so excellent that I am half afraid it might carry the Revised New Testament upon its shoulders into general use. I sincerely hope that this will not happen, for the result would be a decided loss.

However, that is not my point. Returning to our subject, I believe that, on this occasion, the Revised

Version is true to the original. We will therefore use it in this instance, and we will find that it makes good sense. *"I am the good shepherd; and I know mine own, and mine own know me, even as the Father knoweth me, and I know the Father; and I lay down my life for the sheep."*

He who speaks to us in these words is the Lord Jesus Christ. To my mind, every word of Holy Scripture is precious. When God speaks to us by priest or prophet, or in any way, we are glad to hear. When, in the Old Testament, I come across a passage that begins with "Thus saith the Lord," I feel especially blessed to have the message directly from God's own mouth. Yet I make no distinction between one Scripture and another. I accept it all as inspired, and I do not join the dispute about different degrees and varying modes of inspiration, and all that. The matter would be plain enough if learned unbelievers did not mystify it: *"All scripture is given by inspiration of God, and is profitable for doctrine, for reproof, for correction, for instruction in righteousness"* (2 Tim. 3:16).

Still, there is to my mind a special sweetness about words that were actually spoken by the Lord Jesus Christ Himself. These are like honey to me. The words of our text were not spoken by a prophet, a priest, or a king, but by one who is Prophet, Priest, and King in one, even our Lord Jesus Christ. He opens His mouth and speaks to us. You will open your ears and listen to Him, if you are indeed His own.

Notice, also, that not only do we have Christ for the speaker, but we have Christ for the subject. He speaks, and He speaks about Himself. It would not be proper for you or for me to extol ourselves, but there is nothing more pleasing in the world than for Christ to commend Himself. He is different than we are. He is infinitely above us, and He is not under rules that apply to us fallible mortals. When He speaks about His own glory, we know that His words are not prideful. Rather, when He praises Himself, we thank Him for doing so, and we admire the humble graciousness that permits Him to desire and accept honor from such poor hearts as ours. It would be prideful for us to seek honor from men, but it is humility for Him to do so. He is so great that the esteem of inferior beings like us cannot be desired by Him for His own sake, but for ours. Of all our Lord's words, the sweetest are those that He speaks about Himself. Even He cannot find another theme that can excel that of Himself.

Beloved, who can speak fully of Jesus but Jesus? He masters all our eloquence. His perfection exceeds our understanding. The light of His excellence is too bright for us; it blinds our eyes. Our Beloved must be His own mirror. None but Jesus can reveal Jesus. Only He can see Himself, know Himself, and understand Himself; therefore, none but He can reveal Himself. We are very glad that in His tenderness to us He describes Himself with many helpful metaphors and instructive symbols. By these, He wants us to know a little of that love that surpasses knowledge. With His own hand, He fills a golden cup out of the river of His own infinity and hands it to us so that we can drink and be refreshed.

Take these words, then, as being doubly refreshing, because they come directly from the Well

Beloved's own mouth, and they contain rich revelations of His own all-glorious self. I feel that I must quote them again: *"I am the good shepherd; and I know mine own, and mine own know me, even as the Father knoweth me, and I know the Father; and I lay down my life for the sheep."*

In this text, there are three matters that I want to explain. First, I see here complete character: *"I am the good shepherd."* Christ is not a half shepherd, but a shepherd in the fullest possible sense. Second, I see complete knowledge: *"And I know mine own, and mine own know me, even as the Father knoweth me, and I know the Father."* Third, I see complete sacrifice. How preciously that last part concludes the two verses: *"And I lay down my life for the sheep"*! He goes the full length to which sacrifice can go. Let me say that He lays down His *soul* in the place of His sheep; this is the correct translation. He goes the full length of self-sacrifice for His own.

COMPLETE CHARACTER

First, then, our text reveals the complete character of our Lord. Whenever the Savior describes Himself by any symbol, that symbol is exalted and expanded, yet it is not able to convey all of His meaning. The Lord Jesus fills every type, figure, and character; and when the vessel is full, there is an overflow. There is more in Jesus, the Good Shepherd, than you could ever discover from studying a human shepherd. He is the Good, the Great, the Chief Shepherd; but He is much more.

Symbols to describe Him may be multiplied as the drops of dew in the morning, but this multitude will fail to reflect all His brightness. Creation is too small a frame in which to hang His likeness. Human thought is too small, human speech too insufficient, to adequately describe Him. When all the symbols in earth and heaven will have described Him to their utmost, there will remain aspects not yet described. You can force a square to become a circle before you can fully describe Christ in the language of mortal men. He is inconceivably above our ideas, unspeakably above our words.

The Owner of the Flock

Let us think about what Jesus was actually referring to when He described Himself as a shepherd. The shepherd He was talking about is not the type of shepherd that comes to our minds: someone to look after the sheep for a few months until they are large enough to be slaughtered. No, the shepherd in an Oriental society (biblical examples are Abraham, Jacob, and David) is quite another person. The Eastern shepherd is generally the owner of the flock, or at least the son of their owner and therefore their prospective proprietor. The sheep are his own.

On the other hand, Western shepherds seldom, or never, own the sheep. They are employed to take care of them, and they have no other interest in them. In spite of this, the English shepherds I have known are a very excellent set of men as a rule; they have been admirable examples of intelligent workingmen.

Yet, they are not at all like the Eastern shepherd, and cannot be, for he is usually the owner of the flock. The Eastern shepherd remembers how he came into possession of the flock, and when and where each of his sheep were born, and where he has led them, and what trials he has gone through with them. He remembers all this with the added emphasis that the sheep are his own inheritance. The sheep are his wealth. He very seldom has much of a house, and he does not usually own much land. He takes his sheep over a good stretch of country, which is open to everyone in his tribe. But his flocks are his possession. If you were to ask him, "How much are you worth?" he would answer, "I own this many sheep." In Latin, the word for money is related to the word *sheep,* because wool was the wealth of many of the first Romans; their fortunes lay in their flocks.

The Lord Jesus is our Shepherd; we are His wealth. If you ask Him what His heritage is, He will tell you about *"the riches of the glory of his inheritance in the saints"* (Eph. 1:18). Ask Him what His jewels are, and He will reply, "[The believers] *shall be mine...in that day when I make up my jewels"* (Mal. 3:17). If you ask Him where His treasures are, He will tell you, *"The LORD's portion is his people; Jacob is the lot of his inheritance"* (Deut. 32:9). The Lord Jesus Christ has nothing that He values as much as He does His own people. For their sakes, He gave up all that He had and died naked on the cross. Not only can He say, *"I gave...Ethiopia and Seba for thee"* (Isa. 43:3), but He *"loved the church, and gave himself for it"* (Eph. 5:25). He regards His church as

151

being His own body, *"the fulness of him that filleth all in all"* (Eph. 1:23).

The Caregiver of the Flock

The Eastern shepherd, the owner of the flock, is generally also the caregiver. He takes care of the sheep continuously. There is a fireman in my congregation who lives at the fire station; he is always on duty. I asked him whether he was off duty during certain hours of the day, but he said, "No, I am never off duty." He is on duty when he goes to bed, he is on duty while he is eating his breakfast, and he is on duty if he walks down the street. At any time the alarm may sound, and he must do his job and rush to the fire.

In the same way, our Lord Jesus Christ is never off duty. He takes care of His people day and night. He has declared, *"For Zion's sake will I not hold my peace, and for Jerusalem's sake I will not rest"* (Isa. 62:1). He can truly say what Jacob did: *"In the day the drought consumed me, and the frost by night"* (Gen. 31:40). He says about His flock what He says about His garden: *"I the LORD do keep it; I will water it* [or watch over it] *every moment: lest any hurt it, I will keep it night and day"* (Isa. 27:3).

I cannot tell you all the cares a shepherd has concerning his flock, because he has many different anxieties. Sheep have about as many complaints as people. Perhaps you do not know much about them, and I am not going to go into detail, because I do not know much about them myself! But the shepherd knows, and the shepherd will tell you that he leads an anxious life. All the flock is seldom well at one time. One sheep or another is sure to be hurt or sick, and the shepherd spies it out and has eye and hand and heart ready to help and to give relief. There are many varieties of complaints and needs, and all these are laid on the shepherd's heart. He is both possessor and caregiver of the flock.

The Provider for the Flock

Then, he has to be the provider, too, for there is not a woolly head among the flock that knows anything about selecting good pastures. The season may be very dry, and where there once was grass, there may be nothing but dust. It may be that grass is only to be found beside the rippling brooks, here a little and there a little. But the sheep do not know anything about that; the shepherd must know everything for them. The shepherd is the sheep's provider.

Both for time and for eternity, for body and for spirit, our Lord Jesus supplies all our needs out of His riches in glory (Phil. 4:19). He is the great storehouse from which we derive everything. He has provided, He does provide, and He will provide. Every believer may therefore sing, *"The LORD is my shepherd; I shall not want"* (Ps. 23:1).

Dear friend, we often dream that we are the shepherds, or that we, at any rate, have to find some of the pasture. I could not help saying at a recent prayer meeting, "There is a passage in Psalms that says the Lord will do for us what one would have thought we could do for ourselves: *'He maketh me to lie down in green pastures'* (Ps. 23:2)." Surely, if a sheep can do nothing else, it can lie down. Yet, to lie down is the very hardest thing for God's sheep to do. The full power of the rest-giving Christ has to come in to make our fretful, worrying, doubtful natures lie down and rest. Our Lord is able to give us perfect peace, and He will do so if we will simply trust in His abounding care. It is the shepherd's business to be the provider; let us remember this and be very happy.

The Leader of the Flock

Moreover, the shepherd has to be the leader. He leads the sheep wherever they have to go. I was often astonished at where the shepherds in southern France, which is very much like Palestine, take their sheep. Once every week, I saw a shepherd come down to Menton and conduct his whole flock to the beach. Honestly, I could see nothing for them but big stones. Folks jokingly said that perhaps this is what made his mutton so hard. But I have no doubt that the poor creatures got a little taste of salt or something that did them good.

At any rate, sheep follow the shepherd, and away he goes up the steep hillsides, taking long strides, until he reaches points where the grass is growing on the sides of the hills. He knows the way, and the sheep have nothing to do but to follow him wherever he goes. Theirs is not to make the way; theirs is not to choose the path; but theirs is to keep close to his heels.

Don't you see our blessed Shepherd leading your own pilgrimage? Can't you see Him guiding your way? Don't you say, "Yes, He leads me, and it is my joy to follow"? Lead on, O blessed Lord; lead on, and we will follow Your footprints!

The Defender of the Flock

The shepherd in the East also has to be the defender of the flock, for wolves still prowl in those regions. All sorts of wild beasts attack the flock, and the shepherd must run to their aid. So it is with our Shepherd. No wolf can attack us without finding our Lord in arms against it. No lion can roar at the flock without arousing One greater than David. *"He that keepeth Israel shall neither slumber nor sleep"* (Ps. 121:4).

The Good Shepherd

Jesus is our Shepherd, then, and He completely possesses a shepherd's character—much more completely than I can describe.

Notice that the text adds an adjective to the word *shepherd,* adorning our Shepherd with a chain of gold. The Lord Jesus Christ Himself says, *"I am the good shepherd."* He is *"the good shepherd."* He is not a thief; moreover, He is not a shepherd who deals with the sheep only when he takes them from the fold to the slaughter. He is not a hireling; He does not do merely what He is paid to do or commanded to do. Jesus does everything with tender love, with a willing heart. He throws His soul into it. There is a goodness, a tenderness, a willingness, a powerfulness, a force, an energy in all that Jesus does. He is the best possible shepherd.

Again, He is no hireling, nor is He a loafer. Even shepherds that own their own flocks have neglected them, just as there are farmers who do not cultivate their own farms. But it is never so with Christ. He is the Good Shepherd, good up to the highest point of goodness, good in all that is tender, good in all that is kind, good in all the roles in which a shepherd can be needed. He is good at fighting, good at ruling, good at watching, and good at leading. He is surpassingly good in every way.

Notice how Christ puts it: *"I am the good shepherd."* This is the truth that I want to bring out: we can say about other shepherds, "He is a shepherd," but Jesus is *the* Shepherd. All other shepherds in the world are mere shadows of the true Shepherd; Jesus is the substance. After all, what we see in the world with our physical eyes is not the substance, but the type, the shadow. What we do not see with our physical eyes, what only our faith perceives, is the real thing. I have seen shepherds, but they are only pictures to me. The Shepherd—the truest, the best, the surest example of a shepherd—is Christ Himself.

Moreover, you and I are the sheep. The sheep that we may see grazing on the mountainside are just types or symbols of us, but we are the true sheep, and Jesus is the true Shepherd. If an angel were to fly over the earth to find the real sheep and the real Shepherd, he would say, "The sheep of God's pasture are men, and Jehovah is their Shepherd. He is the true and real Shepherd of the true and real sheep." All the possibilities that lie in a shepherd are found in Christ. Every good thing that you can imagine to be, or that should be, in a shepherd, can be found in the Lord Jesus Christ.

Now, I want you to notice that, according to the text, the Lord Jesus Christ greatly rejoices in being our Shepherd. He says, *"I am the good shepherd."* He does not confess the fact as if He were ashamed of it, but He repeats it in the tenth chapter of John so many times that it almost reads like the refrain of a song: *"I am the good shepherd."* He evidently rejoices in the fact. He rolls it under His tongue as a sweet morsel. Evidently, this fact brings great contentment to His heart. He does not say in this passage, "I am the Son of God," or, "I am the Son of Man," or, "I am the Redeemer." But this He does say, and He congratulates Himself on it: *"I am the good shepherd."*

This should encourage you and me to firmly grasp the word *shepherd*. If Jesus is so pleased to be my Shepherd, let me be equally pleased to be His sheep. Let me avail myself of all the privileges that are wrapped up in His being my Shepherd, and in my being His sheep. I see that He is not worried about my being His sheep. I see that my needs will not cause Him any perplexity. I see that He will not be inconvenienced by attending to my weakness and trouble. He delights to dwell on the fact, *"I am the good shepherd."* He invites me to come and bring my needs and problems to Him, and then to look up to Him and be fed by Him. Therefore, I will do so.

Doesn't it make you feel truly happy to hear your own Lord Himself say, and say it to you out of His precious Book, *"I am the good shepherd"*? Don't you reply, "Indeed, You are a good shepherd. You are a good shepherd to me. My heart puts emphasis on the word *good* and says about You, 'There is no one who is good but One, and You are that good One.' You are the Good Shepherd of the sheep"?

We have now looked at the complete character of the Good Shepherd.

COMPLETE KNOWLEDGE

May the Holy Spirit bless our text even more, while I explain the next idea as best as I can.

The knowledge of Christ toward His sheep, and of the sheep toward Him, is wonderfully complete. I must repeat the text again: *"I know mine own, and mine own know me, even as the Father knoweth me, and I know the Father."*

Christ's Knowledge of Us

First, then, consider Christ's knowledge of His own, and the comparison by which He explains it: *"As the Father knoweth me."* I cannot imagine a stronger comparison. Do you know how much the Father knows the Son, who is His glory, His beloved, His other self—yes, one God with Him? Do you know how intimate the knowledge of the Father must be of His Son, who is His own wisdom, yes, who is His own self? The Father and the Son are one spirit. We cannot describe how intimate that knowledge is, yet that is how intimately, how perfectly, the great Shepherd knows His sheep.

He knows their number. He will never lose one. He will count them all in that day when the sheep will *"pass again under the hands of him that telleth* [or counts] *them"* (Jer. 33:13), and then He will total them up. *"Of them which thou gavest me,"* He says, *"have I lost none"* (John 18:9). He knows the number of those for whom He paid the ransom price.

He knows everything about them. He knows the age and character of every one of His own. He assures us that the very hairs on our heads are all numbered (Luke 12:7). Christ does not have a sheep of which He is unaware. It is impossible for Him to overlook or forget one of them. He has such an intimate knowledge of all who are redeemed with His most precious blood that He never mistakes one of them for another or misjudges one of them. He knows their constitutions—those who are weak and feeble, those who are nervous and frightened, those who are strong, those who are presumptuous, those who are sleepy, those who are brave, those who are sick, sorry, worried, or wounded. He knows those who are hunted by the Devil, those who are caught between the jaws of the lion and are shaken until the very life is almost driven out of them. He knows their feelings, fears, and terrors. He knows the secret ins and outs of every one of us better than any one of us knows himself.

He knows your trials—the particular trial that now weighs heavily on you. He knows your difficulties—that special difficulty that seems to block your way. All the ingredients of our lives are known to Him. *"I know mine own...as the Father knoweth me."* It is impossible to have a completer knowledge than that which the Father has of His only begotten Son. It is equally impossible to have a completer knowledge than that which Jesus Christ has of every one of His chosen.

He knows our sins. I often feel glad to think that He always did know our evil natures and what would come of them. When He chose us, He knew what we were and what we should be. He did not buy His sheep in the dark. He did not choose us without knowing all the devious ways of our past and future lives.

> He saw us ruined in the fall,
> Yet loved us notwithstanding all.

Oh, the splendor of His grace! *"Whom he did foreknow, he also did predestinate"* (Rom. 8:29). His election of us implies foreknowledge of all our evil ways. People say that human love is blind. But Christ's love has many eyes, and all its eyes are open, and yet He loves us still.

It ought to be very comforting to you that you are known by your Lord in this way, especially since He knows you not merely with the cold, clear knowledge of the intellect, but with the knowledge of love and affection. He knows you in His heart. You are especially dear to Him. You are approved by Him. You are accepted by Him. He knows you by acquaintance, not by hearsay. He knows you by communion with you. He has been with you in sweet fellowship. He has read you as a man reads a book, and He remembers what He has read. He knows you by sympathy with you, for He is a man like yourself.

> He knows what sore temptations mean,
> For He has felt the same.

He knows your weaknesses. He knows the places where you suffer most, for

> In every pang that rends the heart
> The Man of Sorrows had a part.

He gained this knowledge in the school of sympathetic suffering. *"Though he were a Son, yet learned he obedience by the things which he suffered"* (Heb. 5:8). In all points, He was made like us, and by being made like us, He has come to know us. He knows us in a very practical and tender way.

Suppose that you have a watch, and it will not work, or it works very poorly. Now, suppose that you give your watch to someone who knows nothing about watches, and he says, "I will clean it for you." He will do more harm than good. But then you meet the very person who made the watch. He says, "I put every wheel into its place. I made the whole thing, from beginning to end." You think to yourself, "I have great confidence in this man. I can trust him with my watch. Surely he can repair it, for he made it."

It often encourages my heart to think that since the Lord made me, He can repair me, and keep me repaired to the end. My Maker is my Redeemer. He who first made me has made me again, and will make me perfect, for His own praise and glory. That is the first part of this complete knowledge: Christ's knowledge of us.

Our Knowledge of Christ

The second part is our knowledge of Christ. *"And mine own know me, even as...I know the Father."* You may be thinking, "I do not see much meaning in that. I can see a great deal more meaning in Christ's knowing us." Beloved, I see a great deal in our knowing Christ. That He should know me is great condescension, but it must be easy for Him to know me. Being divine, having such a piercing eye as His, it is not difficult for Him to know me. It is amazingly kind and gracious, but not difficult. The marvel is that I could ever know Him. That such a blind, deaf, dead soul as mine could ever know Him, and could know Him as He knows the Father, is ten thousand miracles in one.

Oh, this is a wonder so great that I do not think you and I have fully realized it yet, or else we would sit down in glad surprise and say, "This proves Him to be the Good Shepherd indeed—not only that He knows His flock, but that He has taught them so well that they know Him!" With such a flock as Christ has, that He should be able to train His sheep so that they are able to know Him, and to know Him as He knows the Father, is miraculous!

Oh, beloved, if this is true of us, that we know our Shepherd, we can clap our hands for joy! I think it is true even now. At any rate, I know enough about my Lord Jesus that nothing gives me so much joy as to hear more about Him. I am not boasting by saying this. It is only the truth. You can say the same, can't you? If someone were to preach to you the finest sermon that was ever delivered, would it please you if there were no Christ in it? No. But you open this book and read about Jesus Christ in words as simple as I can find, and you are satisfied.

> Thou dear Redeemer, dying Lamb,
>   We love to hear of Thee:
> No music's like Thy charming name,
>   Nor half so sweet can be.

Take note that this is the way in which Jesus knows the Father. Jesus delights in His Father, and you delight in Jesus. I know you do, and in this the comparison holds true.

Moreover, doesn't the dear name of Jesus stir your very soul? What is it that makes you desire to be involved in holy service for the Lord? What makes your very heart awake and feel ready to leap out of your body? What but hearing of the glories of Jesus? Play on whatever string you please, and my ear is deaf to it. But once you begin to tell of Calvary, and sing the song of free grace and dying love, oh, then my soul opens all her ears and drinks in the music. Then my blood begins to stir, and I am ready to shout for joy! Right now I want to sing,

> Oh, for this love let rocks and hills
>   Their lasting silence break,
> And all harmonious human tongues
>   The Savior's praises speak.

> Yes, we will praise Thee, dearest Lord,
>   Our souls are all on flame,
> Hosanna round the spacious earth
>   To Thine adored name.

Yes, we know Jesus. We feel the power of our union with Him. We know Him, beloved, so that we will not be deceived by false shepherds. There is a way nowadays of preaching Christ against Christ. It is a new device of the Devil to set up Jesus against Jesus, His kingdom against His atonement, His precepts against His doctrines. The half Christ is preached to frighten people away from the whole Christ, who saves the souls of men from guilt as well as from sin, from hell as well as from folly.

However, these false shepherds cannot deceive us in that way. No, beloved, we can distinguish our Shepherd from all others. We can tell Him apart from a statue dressed in His clothes. We know the living Christ, for we have come into living contact with Him, and we cannot be deceived any more than Jesus Christ Himself can be deceived about the Father. *"Mine own know me, even as...I know the Father."* We know Him by union with Him and by communion with Him. *"We have seen the Lord"* (John 20:25). *"Truly our fellowship is with the Father, and with his Son Jesus Christ"* (1 John 1:3).

We know Christ by our love for Him. Our souls cleave to Him, even as the heart of Christ cleaves to the Father. We know Him by trusting Him. He is *"all my salvation, and all my desire"* (2 Sam. 23:5).

I remember a certain time when I had many questions as to whether I was a child of God or not. I went to a little chapel, and I heard a good man preach. I made my handkerchief wet with tears as I heard this simple workingman talk about Christ and the precious blood. Even while I had been preaching the same things to others, I had been wondering whether this truth was mine, but while I was hearing it for myself, I knew it was mine, for my very

soul lived on it. I went to that good man and thanked
him for the sermon. He asked me who I was. When I
told him, he turned all kinds of colors. "Why, sir," he
said, "that was your own sermon." I said, "Yes, I
know it was, and it was good of the Lord to feed me
with food that I had prepared for others." I perceived that I had a true taste for what I myself knew
to be the Gospel of Jesus Christ. Oh yes, we do love
our Good Shepherd! We cannot help it!

And we know Him also by our shared desires,
for what Christ wants to do, we also long to do. He
loves to save souls, and we love to see them saved.
Wouldn't we win all the people on a whole street if
we could? Yes, in a whole city and in the whole
world! Nothing makes us as glad as the fact that Jesus Christ is a Savior. "Have you read the news in
the paper?" people ask. That news is often of small
importance to our hearts when compared with news
of a spiritual nature.

I happened to hear that a poor servant girl had
heard me preach the truth and had found Christ,
and I confess that I felt more interest in that fact
than in all the rise and fall of political parties. What
does it matter who is in the government, as long as
souls are saved? That is the main thing. If the kingdom of Christ grows, all the other kingdoms are of
small consequence. That is the one kingdom for
which we live, and for which we would gladly die.
Even as there is a boundless similarity of desires between the Father and the Son, so there is between
Jesus and us.

We know Christ as He knows the Father, because we are one with Him. The union between

Christ and His people is as real and mysterious as the union between the Son and the Father.

We have a beautiful picture before us. Can you imagine it for a minute? Picture the Lord Jesus with you. He is the Shepherd. Then, around Him are His own people, and wherever He goes, they go. He leads them to green pastures and beside still waters. And there is this specialness about His people: He knows them as He looks on every one of them, and every one of them knows Him. There is a deeply intimate and mutual knowledge between them. As surely as He knows them, they know Him.

The world does not know the Shepherd or the sheep, but they know each other. As surely, as truly, and as deeply as God the Father knows the Son, so does this Shepherd know His sheep. And as God the Son knows His Father, so do these sheep know their Shepherd. Thus, in one company, united by mutual communion, they travel through the world to heaven. *"I know mine own, and mine own know me, even as the Father knoweth me, and I know the Father."* Isn't that a blessed picture? May God help us to be a part of it!

COMPLETE SACRIFICE

Lastly, our text reveals the complete sacrifice of our Lord. His complete sacrifice is described in this way: *"I lay down my life for the sheep."*

These words are repeated in John 10 in other forms some four times. The Savior kept on saying, *"I lay down my life for the sheep."* Read the eleventh verse: *"The good shepherd giveth his life for the sheep."* The fifteenth verse: *"I lay down my life for the sheep."* The seventeenth verse: *"I lay down my life, that I might take it again."* The eighteenth verse: *"I have power to lay it down, and I have power to take it again."* It looks as if this is another refrain of our Lord's personal hymn. I call this passage His pastoral song. The Good Shepherd sings to Himself and to His flock, and this comes in at the end of each stanza: *"I lay down my life for the sheep."*

Didn't He mean, first of all, that He was always doing so? All His life He was, as it were, laying it down for them; He was divesting Himself of the garments of life until He came to be fully disrobed on the cross. All the life He had, all the power He had, He was always giving for His sheep. This is the first meaning of our text.

It also means that the sacrifice was actively performed. It was always occurring as long as He lived, but He did it actively. He did not just die for the sheep, but He laid down His life, which is another thing. Many a man has died for Christ; it was all that they could do. But we cannot lay down our lives, because they are due already as a debt of nature to God. We are not permitted to die at our own will. That would be suicide and would be wrong. But the Lord Christ's situation was totally different. He was, as it were, actively passive. *"I lay down my life for the sheep....I have power to lay it down, and I have power to take it again. This commandment have I received of my Father"* (John 10:15, 18).

I like to think of our Good Shepherd not merely as dying for us, but as willingly dying—laying down His life. While He had that life, He used it for us, and when the time came, He gave up that life on our behalf. He actually did this for us. When Jesus spoke the words of our text, He had not yet given His life. But now the deed has been done. *"I lay down my life for the sheep"* may now be read, "I have laid down My life for the sheep." For you, beloved, He has given His hands to the nails and His feet to the cruel iron. For you, He has borne the fever and the bloody sweat. For you, He has cried, *"Eloi, Eloi, lama sabachthani?"* meaning, *"My God, my God, why hast thou forsaken me?"* (Mark 15:34). For you, He has breathed His last.

And the beauty of it is that He is not ashamed to declare the object of His sacrifice. *"I lay down my life for the sheep."* Whatever Christ did for the world— and I am not one who would limit the implications of the death of Christ for the world—His particular glory is, *"I lay down my life for the sheep."*

Great Shepherd, do You mean to say that You have died for such as these? What? For these sheep? You have died for them? What? The Shepherd dying for sheep? Surely You have other objects for which to live and die besides sheep. Don't You have other loves, other joys? We know that it would grieve You to see the sheep killed, torn by the wolf, or scattered, but do You really love these poor creatures so much that You would lay down Your life? "Ah, yes," He says, "I would, and I have!"

Carry your wondering thoughts to Christ Jesus. What? Son of God, infinitely great and inconceivably glorious Jehovah, would You lay Your life down for men and women? They are no more in comparison with You than so many ants and wasps—pitiful and pathetic creatures. You could make millions of them with a word, or crush them out of existence by one blow of Your hand. They are weak things. They have hard hearts and wandering wills, and the best of them are no better than they are obligated to be. Savior, did You die for such? He looks around and says, "Yes, I did. I laid down My life for the sheep. I am not ashamed of them, and I am not ashamed to say that I died for them."

No, beloved, He is not ashamed of His dying love. He has told it to His brothers and sisters up in heaven and has made it known to all the servants in His Father's house. This has become the song of that house: *"Worthy is the Lamb that was slain!"* (Rev. 5:12). Shouldn't we join in and sing, *"For thou wast slain, and hast redeemed us to God by thy blood"* (v. 9)?

Whatever people may say about particular redemption, Christ is not ashamed of it. He glories that He laid down His life for the sheep. Note well, it was for the sheep. He does not say "for the world." The death of Christ has an influence on the world. However, in this verse, He boasts and glories in the particular object of His sacrifice: *"I lay down my life for the sheep."*

The verse could even be read, "I lay down my life *instead* of the sheep." He glories in His substitution for His people. When He speaks of His chosen, He makes it His boast that He suffered in their stead—that He bore, so that they would never have to bear, the wrath of God on account of sin. What He glories in, we also glory in. *"God forbid that I should glory, save in the cross of our Lord Jesus Christ, by whom the world is crucified unto me, and I unto the world"* (Gal. 6:14).

Oh, beloved, what a blessed Christ we have who knows us so, who loves us so—whom we also know and love! May others be taught to know Him and to love Him! Yes, may they come and put their trust in Him, as the sheep put their trust in the shepherd! I ask it for Jesus' sake.